Praise for *Buddhism for Mothers*

'Buddhist practitioner Napthali has written an eminently practical book that gives frazzled mothers useable advice and empathy . . . precisely because she is not a teacher and is in the midst of mothering, Napthali offers the approachable and authentic perspective of a rank-and-file practitioner who lives the techniques and situations she writes about.'—*Publishers Weekly*

'Napthali's book focuses on Buddhist practices that will help mothers become calmer and happier in themselves. Follow her advice and we all know what comes next—better parenting.'—*Sunday Telegraph*

'Funny, uplifting, reassuring, real and wise. A truly "mothering" book for mothers . . .'—Stephanie Dowrick

'This is an excellent, practical guide to everyday Buddhism, not just for mothers, but for everyone who has ever had a mother.'—Vicki Mackenzie, author of the best-selling *Why Buddhism?*

'Buddhism for Mothers is an oasis of calm and tranquility in the otherwise chaotic existence that is motherhood.'—*Mind & Body*

'This is Buddhism at its most accessible.'—*Conscious Living*

'. . . approach the day-to-day "highs and lows" differently and more positively, and yes—even more calmly.'—Childbirth Education Association

Reviews from Amazon

'I love this book. It brings such a calming sense of being just by picking it up.'—Kathleen

'The author is very honest and refreshing. On every page you get the sense that the author is a very real person who can relate to both the best and the stressed in us all.'—Suzanne

'IF YOU'RE A MOM, BUY THIS BOOK! I am sceptical of anyone trying to preach an idea to me, and I do not claim to be Buddhist. I just LOVE this book. I checked it out from a local library, but am now purchasing it so I can always have it around. It not only approaches ways to be a calmer mom, but a calmer being in your daily encounter with the world. It has changed how I approach issues, big or small; it's also inspired me to demonstrate the same zen-buddhist coping tools for my children; and it has helped me to stay in the present moment.'—Kristin

Praise for *Buddhism for Mothers with Young Children* (formerly titled *Buddhism for Mothers with Lingering Questions*)

'Napthali is a lovely writer. She skilfully weaves interviews with other parents into her own thoughts. As for guilt, Tibetans don't even have a word for it, she writes.'—*Sydney Morning Herald*

'If you liked her first book, *Buddhism for Mothers*, then you'll adore this one. It'll give you a new perspective on parenting and may even help you enjoy it more.'—*Sunday Telegraph*

'This second book from Sarah Napthali . . . had me repeatedly crying out "yes" . . . By being focused, open and more attentive to the present moment we can enjoy a calmer and happier journey through parenthood; a great companion book for mothers struggling to cope with their new role.'—*Perth Woman*

'There is much here to learn; through Napthali's eyes, patience, reflection and calm become the vehicles to a deeper understanding of self, motherhood and family.'—*Junior*

Praise for *Buddhism for Mothers of Schoolchildren*

'I absolutely loved this book. Many of the teachings of "mainstream" Buddhism are ideas we all understand and appreciate in life—and do not require religious awakening nor a set of orange robes to both appreciate and integrate into our lives . . . If reading *Buddhism for Mothers of Schoolchildren* can bring women anything beyond a strong feeling of empowerment and re-enthusiasm for the beauty of motherhood, it will be the sensation of feeling deeply understood. Of not being alone. Of knowing a few simple shifts in consciousness absolutely have the power to change the direction of a mother's parenting and subsequently the future lives of her precious children.'—www.australianwomenonline.com

'Sarah Napthali's terrific first book *Buddhism for Mothers* showed new mothers how to be calm and contented in the face of the radical shift in their lives. Now Napthali tweaks her Buddhist theories to suit mothers of school-aged children who might be finding that the busy lives of children are taking everyone away from the core values that lead to a fulfilled life.'—*Sunday Mail*

'Warm, wise and engaging, *Buddhism for Mothers of Schoolchildren* is the latest book by Sarah Napthali. Her first two books concentrated on the experiences of mother with babies, toddlers and young children. However, with her children at school, a mother enters a new phase in her life, playing a new role which is a radically different experience from tending the under-fives . . . Written in an accessible and inclusive style, *Buddhism for Mothers of Schoolchildren* is a mindful approach to parenting that helps mothers make the experience of parenting schoolchildren meaningful and spiritual.'—www.femail.com.au

Other books by Sarah Napthali

Buddhism for Mothers

Buddhism for Mothers of Young Children
(previously published as *Buddhism for Mothers with
Lingering Questions*)

Buddhism for Mothers of Schoolchildren

The Complete Buddhism for Mothers
(a compilation of the above three titles)

Buddhism for Parents on the Go

SARAH NAPTHALI

Buddhism
for COUPLES

A CALM APPROACH
TO BEING IN A RELATIONSHIP

inspired
LIVING

ALLEN&UNWIN

First published in 2014

Copyright © Sarah Napthali 2014

Inspired Living, an imprint of
Allen & Unwin
83 Alexander Street
Crows Nest NSW 2065
Australia
Phone: (61 2) 8425 0100
Email: info@allenandunwin.com
Web: www.allenandunwin.com

Cataloguing-in-Publication details are available
from the National Library of Australia
www.trove.nla.gov.au

ISBN 978 1 74331 810 2

Set in 11/15 pt Adobe Garamond Pro by Bookhouse, Sydney
Printed and bound in Australia by Griffin Press

10 9 8 7 6 5 4 3 2 1

contents

introduction

TOMEK LOOKED UP AT me from his breakfast, an apologetic expression on his face, and uttered, 'Oops'.

'What have you forgotten?' I asked, assuming he was about to assign me an errand.

'Connie is getting married next week and I'm supposed to make a speech at morning tea today wishing her well. Any chance you could write a speech and email it to me?'

'But I've never even met Connie!' I blurted. 'What on earth could I say?'

Connie was the personal assistant in Tomek's area at work. Tomek works for a large engineering consultancy so the audience for the speech would be twenty or so engineers and draftsmen, almost all male.

'It only needs to be a minute or two,' Tomek tried to reassure me. 'Just say a few general things about marriage. I need it by ten o'clock this morning if possible.'

Fortunately I have the kind of brain that remembers humorous one-liners so, with only a little help from Google, was able to furnish Tomek with this short, if unoriginal, speech before the ten o'clock deadline.

We are gathered here today because our Connie has decided to live in an institution . . . the institution of marriage, that is.

I highly recommend it . . . so much so that I've done it twice!

I also support gay marriage . . . why should heterosexuals be the only ones to suffer?

To get a woman's perspective, I asked my wife for some advice to give to a woman getting married. She said that marriage teaches you all kinds of personal virtues such as tolerance, patience, forgiveness and lots of other qualities she believes she would never have needed if she hadn't got married.

Yes, there is nothing in the world like the unconditional devotion of a woman . . . It is a thing no married man knows anything about.

But on a serious note, we wish you well Connie for the years ahead and hope you enjoy your honeymoon in Fiji.

I rang Tomek that afternoon to find the speech had elicited a few laughs, although he had excluded the line about gay marriage as a little bleak for the occasion.

Striking that task off my to-do list, I could not suppress a quiet voice inside which inquired, *Is this all I have to say about marriage? All this cynicism? Is there nothing sacred about this bond?*

•

A few years ago, I met a woman called Beth, who was a long-term Buddhist practitioner and marriage counsellor. She told me something about her life with her husband that kept returning to my mind. 'Every night after we finish eating dinner, we join both hands, look into each other's eyes and tell each other things we feel grateful for in our relationship, taking turns. Really simple things like, "I feel grateful that you swept the front porch," or "cooked dinner" or whatever.'

Over the years, I kept recalling this image of Beth and her husband because I found this behaviour so strange. I couldn't imagine doing this if I lived to be a million and three. Yet I could also see that her ritual was a very intelligent, rational and wise act to engage in. It countered one of the most widely cited problems of long-term relationships and one of the leading causes of divorce: lack of mutual appreciation. As a couples counsellor, Beth was in a position to know that expressing gratitude, cultivating what some therapists call 'a climate of appreciation', was one of the best things she could do for her marriage, and, doubtless, her own sense of wellbeing.

I started to think that maybe, in some way, I was blocked. Perhaps, full of blockages. Yet with Buddhist teachings at my fingertips, I knew I had the tools to work on my karmic knots.

•

For years I hesitated to write a book applying Buddhist teachings to the couple relationship. Not least because it might set off my 'imposter syndrome'. Who was I trying to fool that someone like me could write on the topic of adult relationships?

Right now, for example, I have on my desk a cherished book entitled *Everyday Blessings,* about applying Buddhist teachings in family life. A Zen Buddhist couple, Jon and Myla Kabat-Zinn, wrote the book together.

Imagine! My husband doesn't even read my books, let alone write them with me or even show the slightest interest in Buddhism. I do not hold this against him as such behaviours are simply not in his nature and it would be unrealistic—unfair even—for me to expect him to change who he fundamentally is. Still, I could never provide readers with a model of Buddhist marriage like the Kabat-Zinns, whose faces smile at me now from the back-cover photo, a picture of compatibility and shared values.

As the months passed, however, it slowly dawned on me that perhaps, as a woman who has found marriage difficult at times, my perspective on marriage and how to improve its quality could be helpful. After all, when it comes to talking about our relationship worries we tend to gravitate towards people who have experienced similar problems to our own. We may hesitate, for example, to take our relationship problems to friends who appear to live in a perpetual state of marital harmony. Importantly, authors who admit to plenty of difficulties are less likely to make others feel inadequate, inferior or in some way failing.

When I say 'difficult', I do not mean my husband torments me. Not intentionally anyway. My husband is an amazing and impressive man who I admire a great deal, but he could never be called easy-going—his role at work with almost a hundred people reporting to him requires him to be anything but. Our particular challenge is that we have extremely different tastes, opinions, values, hobbies and talents. This isn't to say I believe men are from Mars and women are from Venus. We both come from Earth. (Engineers, however, can be another matter.)

And while I would describe my experience of being married with children as constantly improving, when I think back to those early years with babies, we did start from a low point. Of course, the vast majority of couples struggle in their marriage on the arrival of babies. Karen Maezen Miller, a Zen Buddhist priest and author of a comforting book called *Momma Zen,* eloquently described the shock of a new baby: 'My resentments swelled and crested nearly every day. How unfair the circumstance. How overwhelming the duty. How complete my loneliness as I slogged through the tedium.

I could not fault my tiny daughter these offences; loving her was easy and involuntary. So I faulted my husband. Loving him, you see, was entirely optional. I fortified myself against it with silence and stinginess.'[1]

One hardly needs to read any further to guess that such a clear perception of her situation—'my life is hard; I blame my husband'—was sufficient to slowly begin to heal the relationship. This is the great gift of Buddhist practice: seeing our lives more clearly—through non-judgemental observation—helps us to make changes that benefit everybody.

Along with perceiving our lives more clearly, Buddhist teachings provide other benefits to a relationship. The Buddha offered us the Four Noble Truths:

1. There is suffering, so understand it.
2. The cause of suffering is attachment, so let go.
3. Suffering can end, so realise that it can.
4. There is a path out of suffering, the Eightfold Path.

While I will elaborate on these throughout the book, consider the Second Noble Truth, which is about letting go of attachment or self-centred craving. This teaching can benefit a couple relationship because there are so many attachments we all bring to a partnership that we could let go of. This book will talk, for example, about letting go of anger, of expectations, of unhelpful thoughts and beliefs, and of attachment to our views.

The Buddha's Noble Eightfold Path can also shine considerable light on a couple relationship. This path includes:

1. Skilful understanding
2. Skilful thought

3. Skilful speech
4. Skilful action
5. Skilful livelihood
6. Skilful effort
7. Skilful mindfulness
8. Skilful concentration

With skilful speech, for example, Buddhist teachings can help us develop communication that is sensitive, authentic and conducive to peace. With skilful mindfulness, we can become aware of our thoughts and beliefs about marriage and slowly realise that relationship satisfaction can be, for a large part, 'all in our heads'. We will meet a psychologist who believes that skilful mindfulness can help with a lack of sexual desire. Skilful action is about ethics and avoiding harm which, in the case of marriage, might mean steering clear of an affair or other acts of betrayal.

•

Buddhism has moved from country to country over the centuries and each new culture has produced subtle adaptations, shifts in emphasis and cultural influences. As Buddhism has spread to the West, there have been further adaptations as Western teachers have chosen to emphasise aspects that chime with the democratic, egalitarian principles we value. In the West, we are far less likely to rely on, or become, monks and nuns in order to practise. The quiet, secluded life of traditional, monastic practice in the East gives way to practice amid a complex web of relationships. Western Buddhists focus increasingly on bringing awareness to our relationships, to the quality of our presence with others. Western teachers almost always have partners, and usually children too; celibacy is rare. A large proportion of Buddhist teachers, some say half, are also counsellors or psychotherapists who, for a living, help people navigate relationships.

We can trust that the Buddha would have approved of an emphasis on relationships. On one occasion his attendant Ananda approached the Buddha seeking clarification:

> As he was sitting there, Ananda said to the Blessed One, 'This is half of the holy life, lord: admirable friendship, admirable companionship, admirable camaraderie.'
>
> 'Don't say that, Ananda. Don't say that. Admirable friendship, admirable companionship, admirable camaraderie is actually the whole of the holy life. When a monk has admirable people as friends, companions, and comrades, he can be expected to develop and pursue the Noble Eightfold Path.'

I have seen the 'admirable friendship' of this scripture translated as 'virtuous friendship', 'spiritual friendship' or 'sangha' (the community who help you practise). However we translate the scripture, it suggests that Buddhist practice is about far more than solitary meditation and that relationships, and their capacity to hold a mirror up for us, are crucial to our spiritual development on the path. Many, including myself, would argue that how we interact with others is the ultimate test of spiritual practice. How valuable is it to spend hours in deep meditation if we then treat the people in our lives coldly?

One of the main benefits of Buddhist teachings is that they can change our perspective on our relationship. How easy it is to become caught in a rut where the whole relationship runs on automatic, driven by stale habits. How easy it is to become trapped in circling negative thoughts about our partner. Most of us operate with what psychologists call a 'negativity bias'. Throughout the millennia, focusing on the negative helped us to survive as a species as it helped us deal with danger and all kinds of threats in the environment. Now that we no longer have to worry about coming face to face with a dangerous predator, this negativity bias, while sometimes helpful for identifying problems, can also lead us to relentlessly, and needlessly, focus on the negative. Constantly bracing for the worst blocks the potential for joy and connection. Many of us waste years compiling lists of our partner's faults, ruminating on character flaws, while overlooking a wealth of positive qualities.

Driven by the negativity bias, so many couples reach a stalemate where both claim 'I'm not going to lift my game until she does.' As long as both cling to this stubborn standpoint, as Tomek and I have done at various points in our marriage, there is no hope for the relationship. Sitting around waiting for our partner to change before we allow ourselves to enjoy a loving relationship is a risky, though common, approach. All we can realistically control is our own behaviour, but if we ourselves begin to act more lovingly, it is far more likely that our partner will rise to the occasion.

Of course, many feel apprehensive at the thought of applying Buddhist teachings in their relationship: *Hang on, I'm already doing most of the giving in this relationship. Will Buddhist teachings turn me into a complete doormat? If I become more compassionate, who is going to look out for* my *needs?* Yet whenever Buddhist teachers raise the topic of compassion, they invariably mention the importance of compassion for ourselves, for our compassion needs to encompass all beings, excluding nobody. If our own needs are not being met, then we need to take action to redress the situation by requesting change or setting boundaries. The Buddha himself was pretty unequivocal on this. King Pasenadi and Queen Mallika approached the Buddha to check whether their feelings of love for their own selves over their partner were acceptable. The Buddha replied:

I visited all quarters with my mind.
Nor found I any dearer than myself;
Self is likewise to every other dear;
Who loves himself may never harm another.

For the Buddha, self-interest is natural. We all want to be happy and avoid suffering. Understanding our own self-interest is what helps us avoid violating anybody else's.

As with my past books, I take the unconventional approach of drawing from the three main Buddhist traditions: Tibetan, Zen and Theravadin, even though Buddhists traditionally practise in one tradition only. My excuse is that I remain curious about all three traditions and enjoy investigating each of them. It is for readers to choose which, if any, is right for them. I personally practise in the Theravadin tradition, a form highly influenced by Western teachers, and this feels like home for me.

•

It would be fair to say I reveal rather a lot about my marriage in this book, an area that the great majority of us choose to keep private. In making aspects of my marriage public, I did have to consider the issue of Tomek's privacy. We do have different surnames, though, and I have given him a pen-name for this book. My husband is Polish and Tomek is probably the easiest Polish name to pronounce. I also pledged to show Tomek every sentence that mentioned him, although he soon lost interest and said he trusted me not to defame him.

It has to be said at this point: I married a good man. Some live with partners who may be abusive or even among the 1 per cent of the population believed to be psychopaths. I would hazard a guess that leaving such individuals would help more than applying Buddhist teachings to a lost cause. I am no commitment fundamentalist. My assumption in this book, though, is that readers believe their relationship is probably worth staying in.

The power of Buddhist teachings is that they guide us to delve deeply into our psyches. Through mindfulness and ever-growing self-awareness, they help us to become more familiar with the workings of our minds and bodies, more aware of the thoughts and beliefs that drive our automatic reactions. Assisted to be calm and self-aware for more of the day, we begin to see our behaviour more clearly and our insights gradually help us to relate to our partner more lovingly.

CHAPTER 1

the difficulty of living
as a couple

PICTURE THIS SCENE. A REAL estate agent is conducting a small group tour through a cluster of attractive homes in a recently constructed suburb. After half an hour or so, there is uniform excitement among the group members who are all impressed with these spacious, modern houses set in carefully manicured gardens. The homes are even in the right price range for most of the group and all feel the elation of being close to finding the right home after a lengthy search.

'There is a catch though,' says the agent.

Hearts collectively sink.

'These homes are built on reclaimed swamp so about half of them will eventually sink completely into the mud. It will take a few years though.'

'You can't be serious,' says one of the women.

'I'm afraid I am. And I should also add that a further 20 per cent of the remaining houses will sink quite far down into the mud without completely going under.'

'That's outrageous!' cries one of the men. 'Who in their right mind would buy one of these houses?'

The members of the group all return to their respective homes feeling angry and disappointed. Some decide to write formal letters of complaint to their local member protesting that a scheme with such a high failure rate should even be allowed to exist.

Many an astute reader will have already guessed where I am headed with this tale of real estate woe. The statistics quoted in this scenario are roughly the same as those we hear on the success of modern-day marriage. Here is a rather mind-blowing sample of the proportion of marriages ending in divorce across the Western world:

- United States: 53%
- Australia: 43%
- United Kingdom: 47%

- Germany: 49%
- France: 55%
- Belgium: 71%
- Portugal: 68%[1]

For de facto relationships, separation rates are even higher, the world over.

These statistics only capture the marriages where couples were prepared to go through with a divorce, a procedure widely recognised as one of the most stressful experiences. This begs the question, how many of those not divorced are happily married? A study from the United States suggests that at any given time 20 per cent of those still married are 'in distress'.[2] So a further 20 per cent of houses sink halfway into the mud without completely going under. At least such sinkage is not always permanent.

In the face of such a high failure rate, the lengths we all go to in order to find 'the one' seem curious. Even those who have suffered a divorce remarry at a rate of 75 per cent.[3] Why do we keep signing up to this fate? One reason we often hear is that our quest is a biological drive: without two adults committed to childcare the species would not have thrived. Study after study does reveal, beyond all doubt, that a two-parent family is still the ideal arrangement for raising children.

So although this book may include some depressing stretches, such as most of this chapter (it does brighten up as it goes along), I would argue that knowledge is strength. If we are aware of the reality of what we have all got ourselves into, its pitfalls and traps, then we are in a position to prevent the worst. If we can use Buddhist teachings to reflect on the state of our relationship, then we can protect ourselves from that most stressful of events: relationship breakdown. Not that we are only interested in avoiding the worst: Buddhist teachings can also help strengthen our connection with our partner so that we experience more love and friendship.

Cultivating a Buddhist practice has required me to be honest about my own role in relationship problems. Couples therapists claim that most couples come to counselling in the hope that their partner will finally see their faults and change. In distressed couples, individuals typically blame each other and fail to see their own role in any problems. I remember asking a friend how she was finding the book she was reading on the topic of emotional intelligence. I could only laugh at her answer: 'It's fantastic, I'm really enjoying it,' she enthused. Then with a straight face she added, 'There's just SOOO much in it my husband could learn.'

It's much easier to consider the faults in someone close to us than to see our own. As I have trawled through the literature on relationships, I too have found myself thinking, 'I wish Tomek would read this'. I have even photocopied and bookmarked passages to show him the next time an issue arises. Meanwhile, I suspect I may have overlooked the message in the passages that relate to the parts of me I am reluctant to own up to, my shadow side.

Yet many a couples therapist tells us that while both partners play a part in causing problems, more often than we think it only takes one member of the couple to start making an effort before both benefit and change. I can certainly vouch for this phenomenon in my own relationship with Tomek.

THE FIRST NOBLE TRUTH

The First Noble Truth is simply: 'There is suffering'. The Buddha used the word '*dukkha*', which we tend to translate as suffering, unsatisfactoriness or unease, so it includes all our responses to that which we judge to be unpleasant: irritation, impatience, disappointment, fear, sadness and so on. The most literal translation of the Pali word *dukkha* is a wheel with its axle off-centre. *Dukkha* includes that niggling sense of being off-balance, out-of-kilter, or rickety. For many, the relationship with their partner is an excellent place to start considering this First Noble Truth.

An extended version of the First Noble Truth is: 'There is suffering so understand it'. Buddhist practice requires us to acknowledge *dukkha*, rather than deny, ignore, or pretend that *dukkha* does not exist. The divorce rate alone is evidence that marriage, or any long-term couple relationship, is essentially unsatisfactory, or a source of unpleasant feeling, for substantial periods of time. Diane Sollee, the founder of the Coalition for Marriage, Family and Couples Education in the United States, tells us: 'All couples have approximately ten issues they will never resolve. And if you switch partners you just get ten new issues, and they are likely to be more complicated the second time around.'[4]

At first, ten issues that will never be resolved sounded like an exaggeration, even for Tomek and me. So as I was getting dressed this morning I decided to count the number of issues that Tomek and I are unlikely to ever resolve. I came up with eleven—and thought it best to stop counting there. So it is not hard to prove the First Noble Truth when it comes to living in a couple.

Buddhists talk of '*samsara*', the wheel of suffering that results from living an unconscious life. We experience *samsara* in our relationship when we spend time repeating the same old arguments, falling into the same patterns of disappointment, when we refuse to wake up and see what is going on. We inflict what Buddhists call 'conditioned responses' on each other: the responses we have learnt work for us while growing up, that we believe have helped us to achieve our goals and protected us from hurt. Unaware of just how automatic these responses are, we assume they are inevitable and shut ourselves off from all our options. We live in a trance state, asleep at the wheel. With so much repetition in our interactions, the relationship starts to feel dull, all spark snuffed out. At the worst times, we feel distance, boredom and loneliness.

One way to wake up or reinvigorate the relationship can be to try something different to our conditioned responses, although to do this we need to have noticed that we have fallen into an old pattern. Perhaps our pattern is to see only our own needs and block our partner's from our attention. Our pattern may be to over-talk rather than deliver a concise message, to lose our temper, snipe, nag, complain, bottle up our problems or go quiet and ruminate. Doing something different might mean writing about a grievance in a letter, or even a text, rather than arguing. It could mean expressing gratitude alongside any request for change. Or our new approach may include humour or compassion. It might mean increasing our awareness of how we word our messages, their length, and their clarity.

Buddhism can offer a variety of alternative lenses through which to perceive our relationships, lenses which happily disrupt our habitual ways of seeing. Imagine setting aside a couple of hours as a spiritual exercise—while going about your usual activities—to look at your relationship with nothing but curiosity, with a spirit of calmly inquiring *What is this?*, listening and being open and non-judgemental towards all experience. What a revealing contrast this 'beginner's mind' would be with our habitual lenses.

Alternatively, we could perceive our relationship through a lens of gratitude, focusing on all the benefits we could enjoy if we remain open to them. Another lens is that of compassion, where we ask, 'What is difficult about today for my partner?' and perhaps repeat to ourselves, *May he be at ease*, or *May she be free from strain*. While such Buddhist perspectives can be cultivated in meditation, adopting them throughout our daily activities is surely even more valuable.

Along with trying something different is the option of looking more deeply into our conditioned responses to see what underlies them. So often we find fear: fear of losing control of our surroundings, fear of failing, and fear of not being loved. Seeing our situation more clearly, by challenging ourselves to look deeper, can fuel wiser responses. Antony and Fiona found they disagreed about whether Antony was committed enough as a father. Fiona explains how looking more deeply into her fear helped her to let go:

I've always spent lots of time playing one-on-one with our children. I feel like the main goal of my life is that they know, throughout their entire lives, that they mattered and most of all, that they were deeply loved. Lavishing them with so much attention has felt like a huge commitment for me and I have often felt furious with Antony for not matching my efforts. He definitely adores his children, he's affectionate and does a bit of rough-housing and tickling but he doesn't put in the longer stretches of time reading books, playing games, chatting—which leaves it all to me. It is hard to argue about this when the children are around so I spend a lot of time grumbling to myself about it and this takes its toll on my mood.

I decided to challenge myself to look more deeply at what was going on. I had always been aware that a lot of my attention to my children was a conditioned response to my relationship with my own parents. I came from a large family with really good parents but since my siblings found ways to outshine me I have always felt unsure of whether my parents really loved me. Often, as an adult too, I have felt like a bit of an afterthought for them, as though I'm not on their radar much: they don't think about me very often or remember much about what I'm up to. Although I have few complaints about them as parents I have found my uncertainty about their love for me quite painful and I feel adamant that no child of mine will ever feel that way.

My Buddhist teacher challenged me to use meditation, to get more in touch with unpleasant feelings; not to psychoanalyse myself but just to allow myself to be with the feelings, without pushing them away, without judging them, without adding stories and thoughts. So I sat with the feelings of confusion about my parents' love and was able to notice two emotions. One was sadness but stronger than that was fear. The fear that I don't matter to anyone, that I'm unlovable and also the fear that my children could feel this. My teacher told me that it wasn't a matter of talking myself out of these feelings, as in saying 'But of course you're lovable!' We agreed that was unlikely to work after so many years of feeling that way. I needed to accept that those feelings would arise from time to time and to refuse to empower them by adding thoughts and stories, or doing battle with them. Just notice them: 'Ah, those did-my-parents-really-love-me feelings are here again'.

As for my marriage, I acknowledged that Antony could never understand my fears firsthand because, as a long-awaited son of older parents, he never had cause to question his parents' love for him. I had to admit that my children don't appear to suffer from any lack of time with him and their relationship with him is loving. I needed to accept that Antony, unlike some of our friends, was just not the type to hang out with children for extended periods. Given that he contributes to the household in many other valuable ways, I decided I could loosen my hold on this demand. I might even need to monitor myself in the future to make sure I don't become one of those smothering, over-protective mothers. I decided to express more gratitude for the contribution that Antony does make to the household instead of only focusing on the lack of time he spends doing Lego or playing with them. Nobody can have everything in a partner, I guess.

Any Buddhist teacher will tell you: it is always worth learning more about our fear. So often we fail to acknowledge it and quickly convert it into anger or depression. Rather than be with our fear we rush around, we hide from it, pushing it from our consciousness, becoming increasingly stressed, and this undermines our relationship with our partner.

THE IMPERMANENCE OF A ROMANTIC RELATIONSHIP

One of the reasons there is suffering, according to the Buddha, is that everything is impermanent: nothing stays the same and we don't want to face up to this. Fortunately, impermanence in our relationship works in more than one direction: there will be periods of disintegration but also times when we rediscover contentment, appreciation and warmth.

We often hear of couples who divorce because they 'fell out of love', 'grew apart', or found 'things just weren't the same anymore'. Such explanations show the human resistance to impermanence. For our relationships to have any hope of survival there is a need to accept the Buddha's teaching on the inevitability of change: our relationships, like every other phenomenon, are subject to seasons, to many bouts of changing weather. The only constant in life is change.

When we met our partner we were likely to have felt all the elation of being in love. We probably minimised their faults, idealised their qualities and even invented attractive qualities they did not have. Some of us fell in love with a fiction, a projection of our own desires. Every couple needs to navigate the arduous process of discovering who they really fell in love with, as perceptions based on passion and sexual arousal take second place to a clearer view of our partner.

Relationship researchers distinguish between two approaches to marriage: romantic destiny and relationship growth.[5] Those with a 'destiny' orientation to relationships see their partner as 'the one', their 'soul mate', the person mandated by destiny itself to be their partner in a relationship that was 'meant to be'. Those with a 'growth' orientation, on the other hand, believe that a relationship is something to cultivate, to work on and that it grows stronger through overcoming obstacles. The 'destiny'-oriented fall the hardest when the honeymoon period is over. They feel shocked to find the magic gone and they question whether their partner was really 'the one' after all. They are far more likely to end their relationship. In Buddhist terms, they are attached to an expectation that their relationship will not change. It does not help that so much of popular culture supports a 'destiny' interpretation of love. All the pop songs seem to be about new love rather than the more settled love that becomes the norm for long-term relationships.

The Dalai Lama is in no doubt that the overemphasis on romantic love in Western culture is highly suspect:

> Leaving aside how the endless pursuit of romantic love may affect our deeper spiritual growth . . . the idealization of this romantic love can be seen as extreme. Unlike those relationships based on caring and genuine affection . . . it's something that is based on fantasy, unattainable, and therefore may be a source of frustration.[6]

Since humans are driven to resist change, it can feel tragic, or at least highly disappointing, to find our relationship is no longer passionate or romantic. It is what Buddhists call the suffering of change and it comes from our resistance. The Buddhist path challenges us to practise accepting change, to let go of any clinging to the way things are. Yet there is still plenty of satisfaction available to us, if we can be open to it, from a relationship that has moved on to a more realistic footing.

A well-known model of love comes from psychologist Robert Sternberg, who claimed love has three components: passion, intimacy and commitment.[7] At different stages of a loving relationship, different components are at the fore. While the beginning of a relationship is dominated by passion and intimacy, after a couple of years the relationship shifts to a reliance on commitment and intimacy. The latter form of love, often dubbed 'companionate love', can be just as satisfying as the former but in a different way. It is certainly a form that is more grounded in reality and which provides all the benefits that come with greater emotional stability and a deeper bond.

Back in 1978, American newspapers reported that a senator had awarded Dr Elaine Walster the 'Golden Fleece' award for wasting taxpayers' money. She had conducted a study investigating the differences between passionate love and companionate love.[8] A pioneer at the time, Dr Walster had been researching the topic of love for fifteen years and had interviewed over 100,000 people. In her defence she claimed her findings could help many unhappy couples labouring under the myth that they had missed out on something everyone else had found. Not only was the dissipation of passionate love universal, she found, but fully half her subjects were happier living in companionate love than they had been when in the throes of passionate love. Many had found passionate love too destabilising and intense.

If we know to expect changing phases in our relationship, then we cling less and begin to consider how to make the most of the phase we are in. It also helps to acknowledge that both partners are at some point on the continuum that has connection at one end and autonomy at the other. We both move back and forth on this continuum, sometimes seeking to draw close to our partner and sometimes reclaiming some autonomy. Our movements will not always be in sync with each other but acknowledging the existence of this continuum, and the impermanence of our positions along it, helps us to take less seriously the occasional rebuff from a partner who needs some space.

Sometimes the truth of impermanence works in our favour. In a study of 645 spouses who described themselves as 'unhappily married', two thirds of them ended up 'happily married' when interviewed again five years later. The same study found many happily married spouses had recovered from extended periods of unhappiness even when it was caused by serious problems like alcoholism, infidelity and depression.[9] Sometimes we are simply going through a rough patch that will one day end. It is hard to acknowledge that it will end when we are in the middle of it but many Buddhists console themselves with the words, 'This too will pass'. If we have recently had children, we are highly likely to be going through one of these rough patches that feel endless.

Tomek and I were particularly challenged in our relationship by the arrival of children. Tomek is a neat, orderly type who struggled to cope with the uncontrollability, the unpredictability and the mess. Our babies were constantly vomiting, often screaming, always demanding our undivided attention and in the case of our second-born, Alex, wandering off to explore the world. (We lost him so many times—on two occasions we found him at a Japanese Sushi train restaurant, helping himself to delicacies.) For myself, I struggled to cope with the regimented lifestyle revolving around sleeps and feeds and some dashed expectations around what my husband's role would be. Yet when the children were old enough to be a little more independent, around about school age, the difficulty level eased and that marital rough patch had largely passed.

Another encouraging example of impermanence is the finding that members of a couple tend to grow more similar with time. We are all shaped to some degree by our relationship. After many years together, we have lived through some intense shared experiences that often sculpt us in the same way.[10] Also, the need to live in peace brings us to unconsciously adopt some of our partner's ways and views. This suggests a trend towards more harmony with the passing years. With Tomek's influence, for example, I have greatly improved my critical thinking skills, whereas under my influence he has become more open and receptive to new information.

My friend Andrea captured the impermanence, the changing seasons, of a long-term relationship in an email she sent me recently:

> Marriage is hard. Bloody hard. There are days when I want to drive over him with a truck. But then more and more, I am learning that he is the true definition of a life companion. One that challenges me at the very depth of my being to be better than who I would have been without him.

I, too, was convinced that her husband was worthy of the title 'life companion' on recently learning that although he has proved himself capable of running a double-marathon, he patiently ran alongside Andrea to support her in her first half-marathon.

Like Andrea, we all have the option of learning and growing from the enormous challenges our relationships present to us.

THINGS TO CONTEMPLATE . . .

- Do I fully blame my partner for relationship issues? Do I ever challenge myself to see my own contribution?
- Do I rely on nagging, criticism, sulking or yelling to improve things and, if so, what are some more skilful ways to address our problems?
- Do I accept that every marriage has its unresolvable issues to live with? Is there anything I can afford to let go of trying to control or change?

- Have I ever thought creatively about different ways to address problems or do I fall back on the same old habitual behaviours?
- Am I wasting hours of my short, precious life ruminating? If so, what would I have to do to reduce or stop this?
- Have I looked deeply at what might underlie my habitual responses? Any unmet needs, childhood issues, fears?
- Do I believe my partner needs to be 'the one', my 'soul mate' who was 'meant to be' for me? Could I shift my perspective to a more flexible one that allows for inevitable periods of ill-will between us?

THINGS TO DO

- Understand that any couple relationship will have periods of great difficulty, that this is natural and universal.
- Accept impermanence, that a relationship has seasons. Feelings of intimacy, love, irritation and even hatred will come and go.

CHAPTER 2

letting go

A WELL-KNOWN TALE FROM Zen Buddhism goes like this:

> A senior monk and a junior monk were on a pilgrimage together
> when they came to a rapid-flowing river. Beside it, a beautiful
> woman was weeping. Unable to swim, she was afraid to cross
> it alone. She asked if the monks could help her to cross it. The
> senior monk hoisted the woman onto his shoulders and carried
> her across the river before bidding her farewell. Two hours later,
> the senior monk noticed that the junior monk was quiet and
> frowning so asked him why. The junior monk replied: 'You broke
> our rules when you carried that woman across the river. We are
> not allowed to touch a woman.' The senior monk replied: 'Are
> you *still* carrying that woman? *I* put her down two hours ago!'

I often think of this story when I find myself, like the junior monk,
dwelling on the past wrongdoings of others. It is also a lesson in how
being attached to our views, like the junior monk was attached to
his rules, can obstruct our ability to respond wisely to our current
circumstances.

The Second Noble Truth is that the cause of suffering is attachment. That is to say, when we cling or grasp to what is impermanent,
in the service of our deluded sense of what is 'I, me and mine', then we
suffer. The extended version of the Second Noble Truth is: 'The cause
of suffering is attachment, so let go.' Letting go of attachments, the
Buddha taught, is the path out of *dukkha*. Let's consider, for example,
letting go of our attachment to our expectations of our relationship.
That is not to say that we become doormats who do not defend
our rights and interests, but rather that we hold our expectations as
preferences rather than as demands that torment us.

In her book *Committed*, which explores the nature of marriage
over time and across cultures, Elizabeth Gilbert finds herself in

Northern Vietnam where she interviews some women from the Hmong community, who are traditional mountain people. Her various questions about marriage—'What do you believe is the secret to a good marriage?', 'Is your man a good husband?'—were met by either riotous laughter or confusion, leaving Gilbert to ponder what was behind these reactions. She concluded: 'Meeting the Hmong that day in Vietnam reminded me of an old adage: "Plant an expectation: reap a disappointment." My friend the Hmong grandmother had never been taught to expect that her husband's job was to make her abundantly happy . . . Never having tasted such expectations to begin with, she had reaped no particular disenchantment from her marriage.'[1]

The Hmong are by no means the only ethnic group with a purely pragmatic approach to marriage. It is peculiarly Western to expect as much as we do from our partners. The modern Westerner expects romance, emotional support, friendship, great sex, stimulating conversation, shared parenting and on and on goes the list. Surely this is too much for one relationship to bear. Moreover, we have only been expecting so much for the past two hundred years of human history. Even Westerners, for most of our history, have married for pragmatic reasons related to finances and status. So our high-expectation approach is not only unique to Westerners, but also relatively new. And the high divorce rates suggest it is not working.

A study of marital satisfaction in India over a ten-year period compared arranged marriages with non-arranged marriages. Just as we experience in the West, there was a dramatic decrease in romantic love over the ten years for those who married for love. Those in arranged marriages, however, experienced a large and steady increase in romantic love. At the five-year mark, the level of romantic love in arranged marriages overtook the level experienced in the non-arranged marriages, and far surpassed the non-arranged marriages by the ten-year mark.[2] While Westerners will never opt for arranged marriages, these findings suggest that the expectations stimulated by marrying for love are a threat to marital satisfaction. It can be liberating to let go of them, as this mother found:

I have spent most of my marriage feeling bitter that my husband has failed to provide emotional support. I've always told myself that providing sympathy, being there for me when I'm down, is absolutely fundamental to a halfway decent marriage and all my friends agree with me. Then, after about fifteen years of marriage, I visited my husband's home town and met some of his siblings who I had never met before. I had always known that my husband didn't like his father but he had never shared too many details about their relationship. One of his brothers is very open and talks a lot and that is how I learned, after fifteen years of marriage, that my husband's father was actually a violent man, who beat not only his wife but also his children. I had no idea that my husband had experienced such hardships. I felt sad for my husband's difficult childhood but I also found myself looking anew at our relationship.

Back home, I talked with my husband about his childhood and he opened up, although not much. What shocked me most was his lack of emotion around what happened to him as a child. Suddenly, my marital problems made sense. My husband had learnt, had been forced to learn, to shut off his emotional side at a very young age. While he was capable of impatience, irritation and anger, he seemed closed to emotions like sadness, and that included feeling sad for the hardships of others. I finally understood that he would always struggle to be there for me when I felt down because he had lost the ability to even be there for himself in times of sadness.

I actually felt liberated: I could let go of an expectation that had been making me miserable. While my husband meets many of my needs and we generally enjoy each other's company, he will never provide emotional support of the kind I've wanted and now I can understand why and accept that. I would have to go to others, or just rely more on my own inner resources, for emotional support. I can live with that.

As an antidote to our over-reliance on a romantic partner to fulfil so very many needs, we can take measures to increase the amount of support we give and receive from other sources than solely our partner. The Dalai Lama, who claims never to feel lonely, recommends that we aim for closeness with as many people as possible based on our shared humanity:

> I've never felt a lack of people with whom I can share things . . .
> It's easy for me to share things with others; I'm just not good at
> keeping secrets! . . . and it's not just a matter of knowing people
> and having a superficial exchange but of really sharing my deepest
> problems and suffering.[3]

Although we cannot suddenly become just like the Dalai Lama, his words remind us of the potential to connect deeply with so many more people than only our partner. I find it interesting that he portrays himself as so ready to self-disclose, for I have read many times that lonely people avoid self-disclosure. Sharing information about ourselves is one of the important keys to connecting and finding intimacy. That said, the Buddha's instructions about Skilful Speech suggest we share judiciously: our disclosures to others need to be to 'the right person' at 'the right time and place' on 'the right subject'.

LETTING GO OF THE NEED FOR A PARTNER TO COMPLETE US

Among the most divorce-prone relationships are those that experience a pattern called 'demand–withdraw', also referred to as the 'pursuer–distancer' pattern. In these relationships one partner, typically the woman, seeks more intimacy, support, attention or respect by criticising, nagging or demanding. The other partner, typically the male, responds with conflict-avoiding behaviours such as withdrawal, defensiveness or silence. It is typically a vicious cycle where each partner's behaviour only reinforces the others' until they both feel wretched and dissolution of the relationship is increasingly likely.[4] While many diagnose the demand–withdraw pattern as a problem of communication styles, it also springs from the needs, or even the neediness, of the demander.

The Buddha's final words were:

Be a light unto yourself; betake yourselves to no external refuge.
Look not for refuge to anyone besides yourselves.

Many of us believe—and we may not even be conscious of our belief—that others exist for the purpose of fulfilling our needs. Such a belief brings us to approach our relationship with our partner in a grasping, cloying fashion. We all turn to others to attend to some of our needs as humans, to ward off loneliness, and we feel disappointed when they fail to deliver. After all, even if we did find someone who removed some of the pain of life, their power to do so would not be consistent over time nor would it last forever.

Buddhist practice can help give us strength and autonomy. It provides tools, such as meditation and mindfulness, which help us soothe ourselves and manage upsetting thoughts, so that we require less from those around us. Perhaps, for example, our partner meets many of our needs but is not too strong on empathy: they may be more of a fixer than a listener. Yet when we develop our own capacity for self-compassion, along with our tolerance for the less pleasant emotions, we demand less from the relationship and reduce the potential for resentment.

We need to see ourselves as whole on our own, rather than expecting a partner to complete us. Indeed, the Zen view is that we are already whole, right now, in this very moment. Sure, we have some delusions and attachments to let go of in order to enjoy this wholeness. Yet we all have enormous potential to cultivate the inner resources that help us manage our emotions, that help us accept ourselves for how we are, and that allow us to experience more gratitude and contentment with our lives.

SELF-COMPASSION

Psychotherapist Subhana Barzaghi is a senior Buddhist teacher in the Zen as well as the Theravadin tradition: 'In the Christian culture most of us grew up in, we learnt that it was self-indulgent, narcissistic even, to love yourself. But our love for our own self, in fact, needs to be one hundred per cent. No less. That means for every part of ourselves, warts and all.' This might at first sound like a tall order, but isn't this the kind of love we already have for our children? Would it be so hard to channel some of this infinite love to ourselves? For me, the teachings on self-love have been among the greatest treasures of Buddhist practice. If we can apply to ourselves what the Buddha refers to as 'the love of a mother for her only child' then we enter into a nurturing relationship with ourselves instead of that of the harsh judge berating the wayward child. I particularly benefit from this teaching during meditation where I consciously relax the inner critic and let the inner mother come forward and be there for me. This makes for a peaceful, calm and soothing sit.

Kristin Neff, an associate professor at the University of Texas, was so inspired by the power of self-compassion that she conducted pioneering research and wrote a book called *Self-compassion: The proven power of being kind to yourself.*

When I first came across the idea of 'self-compassion', it changed my life almost immediately . . . I was going through a really difficult time following the breakup of my first marriage, and I was full of shame and self-loathing. I thought signing up for meditation classes at a local Buddhist center might help . . . I had known that Buddhists talk a lot about the importance of compassion, but I had never considered that having compassion for yourself might be as important as having compassion for others. From the Buddhist point of view, you have to care about yourself before you can really care about other people. It took me a while to get my head around it. But I slowly came to realize that self-criticism—despite being socially sanctioned—was not at all helpful, and in fact only made things worse. I wasn't making myself a better person by beating myself up all the time. Instead, I was causing myself to feel inadequate and insecure, then taking out my frustration on the people closest to me. More than that, I wasn't owning up to many things because I was so afraid of the self-hate that would follow if I admitted the truth.

What [my new partner] Rupert and I both came to learn was that instead of relying on our relationship to meet all our needs for love, acceptance, and security, we could actually provide some of these feelings for ourselves. And this would mean that we had even more in our hearts to give to each other.

We were both so moved by the concept of self-compassion that in our marriage ceremony later that year, each of us ended our vows by saying 'Most of all, I promise to help you have compassion for yourself, so that you can thrive and be happy.'[5]

Kristin went on to run a regular eight-week program, called Mindful Self-compassion, to teach self-compassion skills.

The overemphasis in our culture on romantic love—in our pop songs, magazines, movies and fiction—probably contributes to a habit in many of us to look to others instead of ourselves for the love we need. When we love ourselves fully, we don't need to follow our partner around pleading with them to do it for us. We remove clinging, grasping attachment from the relationship and reduce the potential for *dukkha*. Of course, it is wonderful if our partner can provide this kind of deep love for us but we cannot afford to rely on their love alone. Like everything, their love for us will change in its nature and expression many times over the course of a relationship.

This is not to say that we should put up with a relationship that is low in warmth, support and kindness and pretend to be completely self-contained. The Buddha, based on his experiences of both overindulging in sensual pleasures and then starving himself, decided that 'the middle road' between extremes worked best. So while we do what we can to shape our relationship into one of mutual caring, we also aim to be strong enough to provide our own self-assurance rather than expecting too much from our partner. If we continue to feel down on ourselves for an extended period, despite our best efforts to lift our spirits, then a qualified therapist or wise friend is likely to be more helpful than most partners.

THE TRUTH ABOUT THE SECOND NOBLE TRUTH

The cause of *dukkha* is attachment, according to the Buddha, but there is one root attachment at the centre of all the trouble and that is the attachment to the self. We see ourselves as an entity separate from others, separate from every object in the world, yet the Buddha taught that this perception is a delusion which makes us suffer. Not only do we feel ourselves to be cut off from others but we assume we are a fixed, unchanging self who behaves consistently across situations and over time.

Seeing ourselves as coherent, in a way that 'makes sense', gives us a sense of certainty with which to go forward into the world, but we rarely consider the costs of this illusory self we have constructed. For starters, when you have a carefully constructed self, you must put a lot of energy into defending it, protecting its interests and collecting materials and achievements to enhance it. You define it in a way that limits its scope for development: I'm this type of person, not that type.

When we investigate our relationship with this 'self' we realise that it takes up a lot of our mental space, and seems to be the crux of all our most damaging preoccupations. *Am I good enough? Am I loved enough? Have I achieved enough? How do others perceive me? Am I too x or too y?* With investigation, we notice that when we are at our most vulnerable, the sense of self is at its strongest, its most exaggerated. We feel certain of a 'me under siege'. If we could let go of the attachment to self, then the suffering could end. And this is the Third Noble Truth: *dukkha* can end. Some Buddhists argue that it can end once and for all, as it did for the Buddha who became enlightened. Many in the West prefer to interpret the Third Noble Truth less absolutely, as meaning that suffering can end in any moment we choose to let go of an attachment.

During the worst times, we use our relationship with our partner to reinforce our false sense of self. We feel a strong sense of separation from our partner: our interests are opposing, his gain is my loss and vice versa. We compete: me versus you. No 'we'. No 'us'. We keep score: I did more housework and childcare than you, I had a harder day, I have a tougher life. We see only differences, and overlook our common humanity. We fuel the false sense of separation, which in turn fuels our *dukkha*, our experience of life as unsatisfactory and painful.

In her book *Lovingkindness* Sharon Salzberg, a Buddhist teacher widely described as one of the elders of Western Buddhism, wrote: 'When we experience a strong idea of separate, immutable self and other, it seems as though there is constantly a great big "other" out there. To bear this danger, we need to hold ourselves in tense readiness, waiting for every impact . . . Seeking only to protect ourselves, we cannot genuinely connect with others . . . and we struggle with terrible aloneness.'[6] During times of relationship conflict or rumination on the injustices, it helps to turn our attention inward, asking ourselves, *How is my sense of self right now?* The answer for me at such times has always been 'mighty strong', which means it is highly exaggerated and therefore causing a lot more trouble than it needs to.

Like other Buddhist friends, I find it helps to adopt a mantra that challenges the false sense of self, the words of the Buddha, *This is not me, this is not mine, this is not myself.* This stops us taking everything that happens to us so personally. It is not about me. Whatever moment we find ourselves in is the result of a long stream of causes and conditions, many of which have very little to do with the self that I so strongly believe in. If we stop frantically protecting and defending the self, taking the self ever so seriously, we can get on with some real problem-solving, and some authentic relating.

THINGS TO CONTEMPLATE . . .

- Given the impossible number of needs our culture leads us to expect a partner to fulfil, which expectations could I let go of, or hold more loosely?
- Do I rely on the approval, or affection, of others in order to feel like a worthwhile human being? Or can I provide my own self-acceptance?
- Do I practise self-compassion? Do I love myself one hundred per cent? (It is harder to provide love and acceptance to others when we can't provide it for ourselves.)
- How much do I suffer from the delusion of 'self and other'? Do I feel completely separate from my partner? Do I have an exaggerated sense of a separate, unchanging 'self'? Do I find it needs a lot of defending and maintenance work?

THINGS TO DO

- Cultivate connections with friends and family other than our partners to reduce the emotional load on one person. If you are naturally reserved, consider sharing more of yourself with others and making space for others to do the same with you.
- Validate yourself rather than expecting your partner to do it.
- When you notice your sense of self is exaggerated, try the Buddha's mantra: *This is not me, this is not mine, this is not myself.*

CHAPTER 3

mindfulness of our thinking

IF YOU BELIEVE THE Buddha, it is important to pay attention to the role our thoughts play in our lives rather than leave them unguarded. Consider these quotations from the Buddha about thoughts. I personally consider each one of these quotations incredibly powerful and worth recalling at every opportunity.

With our thoughts we make the world.

Who is your enemy? Mind is your enemy.
Who is your friend? Mind is your friend.
Learn the ways of the mind. Tend the mind with care.

Your worst enemy cannot harm you as much as your own unguarded thoughts.

For me, one of the greatest benefits of Buddhist practice has been the way it has changed my relationship with my own thoughts. You see, I used to believe my thoughts. I had to act on them, because they were true. I always assumed they were helping me solve problems and improve my life. If I just kept thinking, I would be able to engineer a life full of pleasure, devoid of pain. I believed it was possible to think my way out of every discomfort, dilemma or debacle. In retrospect, I wonder why I allowed my thoughts to carry such weight. Thoughts are like bubbles: insubstantial, arising from nowhere and vanishing into nowhere. They are mere scraps of language, random images and sounds.

With exposure to Buddhist teachings, I learned to bring awareness to my thinking processes. I noticed my thoughts were highly repetitive and prone to fixation and obsession. I began to recognise the same boring old themes constantly arose. If I was tired, many of the thoughts were grumbling and cranky in nature. The feeling tone of my thoughts, that is, whether they were cheering or depressing, seemed to depend on my physical state or my mood. I could only conclude that the majority of my thoughts were highly unreliable, and not worth trusting. Sometimes they were helpful, but mostly I needed to keep a close eye on them.

I decided to learn more about my thought patterns and ask whether a pattern of thought sabotaged me or helped me. The Buddha encouraged us to study our thought patterns but he specified a particular way to approach the task. He recommended bringing 'bare attention' to them, which is to say, bare of judgement. The attention we bring to our thoughts needs to be non-reactive, non-judgemental, receptive and open.

For instance, compare the first and the second example:

Example 1: '[My partner] forgot to call me today. That makes me feel like I don't matter to him.'

Example 2: '[My partner] forgot to call me today. That makes me feel like I don't matter. Why am I so needy? I should be strong and self-reliant. I hate how he makes me feel this way—it's his fault. Now I feel angry and I hate being angry. I feel guilty for getting angry because anger is bad. And now I feel sad that I feel guilty because I feel like a general failure. Bugger, we're out of chocolate . . .'

In the first example, we observe the thought and the unpleasant feeling that accompanies it but instead of judging our thought, or judging ourselves for having the thought, we allow ourselves to simply experience it. We make room for the thought, and the accompanying feeling, and we do so with an attitude of compassion and kindness for ourself. We practise being with our current state, without adding anything.

In the second example, we are not mindful: we judge our thoughts and feelings. Instead of some mild sadness, we are overwhelmed with regret, then anger, then guilt, then more sadness, then craving for chocolate. We could have short circuited the whole process by accepting our initial thought, and its accompanying feeling, without judgement.

The first approach doesn't mean the sad feeling will instantly go away. It may, or it may not, but when we notice our thoughts and refrain from judging them, we don't waste our emotional energy struggling against them. This frees up mental space for more constructive activity. While practising mindfulness of our thoughts, we will notice plenty of thoughts that we don't like and would rather be free of, but if we struggle against them we only give them more power than if we simply let them be, aiming only to 'notice'.

Many psychologists will advise us to dispute our negative thoughts, collecting evidence for why they are not realistic. This approach comes from Cognitive Behaviour Therapy. More recent therapies, however, suggest we don't bother with the disputing and that we just allow the unhelpful thoughts to run their course, be aware of them, but leave it there: allow them to exist without any struggle against them. This is the strategy used in Acceptance and Commitment Therapy, and in Mindfulness-based approaches.

I must say I have felt encouraged in my spiritual practice to find psychologists now offer therapies that resemble what the Buddha taught over 2500 years ago. It is especially encouraging that a large amount of empirical evidence into such therapies supports claims they are effective in treating depression and anxiety.[1]

Of course, often enough we do not deal with only one thought, as in the example I gave above, but whole stories, revenge fantasies or escapist daydreams. We may have spent minutes, or hours, lost in ruminative, mindless thought. The moment we realise this, however, is the moment we 'wake up'. The moment of clarity, where we realise we were not paying bare attention, is the moment of liberation.

This is the Buddha's Third Noble Truth: suffering, or *dukkha*, can end in any moment. Every moment of our lives is an opportunity to wake up and be mindful, to open ourselves to bare attention and let go of habitual, automatic reactions. The skill of waking up to the present moment is one that Buddhists practise, for it empowers us to intercept our karma and change direction.

Given that our thinking in relation to our long-term relationship with our partner can be so automatic and habitual, it is nothing short of exciting to have the option of mindfulness available to us. With non-judgemental awareness of how we habitually think about our relationship, so much can change. And if we can bring mindfulness to our interactions as well, then the possibilities for relationship-repair, appreciation and love multiply. As one psychology lecturer I know always says: *relationship happiness is all in our heads*. While this wouldn't be true for a victim of domestic violence, for my relationship—and hopefully yours—I think she is, to a larger extent than we routinely care to admit, right.

Two arrows

The Buddha taught that most of our suffering is self-created. This means that we are all in a position to drastically reduce the amount of suffering, or dis-ease, we experience. In life, the Buddha explained, we can be hit by two different types of arrows. The first arrow is inevitable: we will all experience, for example, physical pain. The second arrow is the arrow we direct at ourselves and we can see it as our reaction to the first arrow. Rather than suffer only the first arrow of physical pain we send ourselves 'second arrows', such as when we add: *Why does this always happen to me?*, *I don't deserve this*, *What if the pain continues for a long time?* and so on.

Hence, we hear many a Buddhist teacher declare: 'Pain is inevitable; suffering is optional'.

The analogy of the two arrows does not only apply to physical pain. If our partner appears to ignore us, if we sense disrespect, then it is inevitable we feel the pain of a first arrow. Humans have evolved to be sensitive to any hint of rejection, given that such behaviour, throughout the ages, was literally a threat to our survival: if we did not fully belong to a tribe, then our needs for protection and food would go unmet. The brain regions activated when we are in physical pain are the same regions activated when we suffer the feelings evoked by ostracism.[2] Yet if we are mindful of our thinking after an incident where our partner has tried to create distance, we notice ourselves throwing numerous second arrows: *He doesn't care about me, How do I put up with such insensitivity?, He* always *does this.*

Modern-day psychologists talk about attributions, or the causes we come up with to explain others' behaviour. When responding to our partner's behaviour, we choose between an interpretation that supports the relationship or one that undermines it. Let's consider the example of Tomek and I, who have shown a potentially disturbing tendency to forget each other's birthday until the day is well advanced. While neither of us are interested in gifts we would both still appreciate some recognition on our birthday.

Psychologists identify five dimensions in which we make attributions.[3] In each case, it is easy to tell which attribution enhances the relationship and which undermines it. In the case of my forgotten birthday, I have some choices in how I interpret Tomek's behaviour:

- I can make an **internal** attribution that relates to Tomek's internal world (*Tomek is forgetful, self-absorbed*) or an **external** one (*Tomek has many demands on him at work*).

- I can make a **stable**, ongoing attribution (*Tomek always forgets my birthday*) or an **unstable**, temporary one (*He did remember last year*).
- I can see the event as **controllable** (*He should have written it in his diary*) or **uncontrollable** (*It's hard to remember these details when you're very busy*).
- I can judge the behaviour to be **global**, part of Tomek's character as a whole (*My husband is inconsiderate, selfish*), or **specific** to the situation (*Of course he forgot, given he had that huge presentation to deliver*).
- I can tell myself the offence was **intentional** (*He did it to rile me*) or **unintentional** (*He didn't mean any harm*).

A short way of checking up on our attributions if we fail to memorise the five dimensions above, is to simply ask ourselves: *Did I give my partner the benefit of the doubt or did I assume the worst?* We may delude ourselves that we punish our partners when we choose destructive attributions but we tend to punish ourselves far more because such attributions upset us and deprive us of relationship satisfaction. Sadly, researchers have found that adults who had insecure relationships with their parents as very young children are more likely to come up with upsetting attributions as adults.[4] If, on the other hand, we practise mindfulness of our thoughts and recognise when we are needlessly inventing destructive attributions, we empower ourselves to block those second arrows, or at least take them less seriously, no matter what our background.

One interesting phenomenon psychologists note is that when making attributions about our own behaviour we are highly aware of all the extenuating circumstances, the myriad potential reasons for our actions. When making attributions about others, however, it is so easy to portray them as two-dimensional characters whose actions arise from their flawed personality rather than all the complexities of their situation. This reflects what is called our 'self-serving bias'. Something for the mindful to look out for.

Awareness of unhelpful beliefs

If we practise mindfulness of our thinking, we are likely to notice some of our beliefs. Often enough, some of our beliefs are not worth holding on to. One good reason to let go of any of the beliefs about relationships that I list below is that although these beliefs are common, they are not supported by the evidence.

'Conflict is bad'

On an emotional level, conflict certainly feels bad and can give us the impression that our relationship is failing but to suppress conflict, or pretend everything is rosy, is to ignore the Buddha's First Noble Truth: there is suffering, stress and unsatisfactoriness. The widely quoted relationship expert John Gottman, who has studied the relationships of hundreds of couples, argues it is not whether we experience conflict that determines marital satisfaction but how we handle it. In successful marriages, spouses do engage in conflict rather than leaving irritations unresolved, but they use more skilful communication to do so than the less successful couples. For example, they avoid expressions of contempt and criticism.[5]

'We are the only couple that fight'

When we see other couples in social contexts, all looks cheery, and we think to ourselves that we are the only couple harbouring smouldering resentments. In our darkest moments, we convince ourselves that everyone else is getting on just fine in their relationships. We wallow, thinking, 'I alone suffer'. To quote from a study of 778 married couples in Detroit: 'nearly everyone reports at least an occasional disagreement, with the typical respondent reporting one to two disagreements per month'.[6]

'Partners cannot change'

To deny change is as close as one can come to blasphemy in Buddhism. If there is one thing we all do, it is change. Such a belief could render us defeatist so that we settle for a dull relationship or stop making any effort. Then there is the Third Noble Truth: suffering can end, anytime we are, or our partner is, prepared to let go of attachment. I am reminded, however, of the joke, 'How many social workers does it take to change a light bulb?' The answer: 'None, the light bulb has to want to change itself'. We cannot force our partner to change; we can only work on ourselves. Whatever annoys us about our partner will eventually change, maybe subtly, maybe dramatically, or maybe our own attitude towards the annoying characteristic in our partner will change.

'Men and women come from different planets'

Speak to any psychology academic about the blockbuster *Men are from Mars, Women are from Venus* and I guarantee they will slam it as the ultimate example of pop psychology. At least, the handful of psychology academics I have met share this view. (Despite the views of academics, I have met people who swear that the book 'saved their marriage'.) Believing that the two genders are so incredibly different when they are not is not helpful, as we overlook important similarities that could help us to connect. 'Sex differences in intimate relationships tend to be much less noteworthy and influential than laypeople often think,' to quote from one psychology textbook. It also says: 'It's more work, but also more sophisticated and accurate, to think of individual differences, not sex differences, as the more important influences on interpersonal interaction.'[7]

My relationship with Tomek smashes plenty of gender stereotypes: he is neater, cleaner, more capable of multi-tasking, more fond of shopping, more interested in clothes, more conscious of physical appearance in self and others, more observant of his surroundings and what needs attending to. I am more likely to seek distance and 'retreat into my cave' than he is. He is more particular about how to do household chores. He is the one to make a list of jobs for me rather than I for him. I'm more likely to be the 'fun parent' or hang out at the park with the kids while he attends to odd jobs. I crack more jokes. He is more responsible about planning for our future and attending to important household issues.

•

To this list I can add a belief of my own that needed dispelling. During the hard times in my marriage, I have caught myself thinking: *I'm just not cut out for this whole marriage thing*. My thoughts run along the lines that marriage is just too damaging to my autonomy, my time alone, my freedom. *I'm just hanging in there for the kids*, says my inner martyr.

Yet studies of tens of thousands of adults across the Western world, in many ethnic groups, over many decades, have all delivered the same finding: people in couples are significantly happier than those who are not. They also enjoy better physical and mental health, higher immunity, lower rates of depression and suicide, better recovery rates from life-threatening diseases and higher life expectancies.[8] This suggests my belief, on bad days, that I am not designed for marriage is a delusion.

If I cast my mind back to the two or three years that I was single in my late twenties, I have to admit that while I was perfectly happy living alone from Monday to Friday, I would start to feel lonely come the weekend. While for most of my life I have favoured listening or turn-taking in conversations, when I lived alone I subjected anyone who phoned to a monologue of all my unspoken thoughts. Now with a long-term partner, there is someone to share such thoughts with: I have a pleasant conversation at breakfast with Tomek every morning before the boys wake up, we phone each other briefly throughout the day, and chat at day's end. We take all this interaction for granted, as part of the routine, and forget to value it, but if we were to lose one another this regular interaction would be painful to forgo.

If I continued to entertain the belief that I'm only married for the sake of the children, I could one day be one of those widows who lament that she never recognised the treasure she had until it was too late. That might sound melodramatic but this happens: widows and widowers can experience tremendous grief after even a 'passionless' marriage, having never recognised the numerous ways their routines were 'meshed' together.[9]

THINGS TO CONTEMPLATE . . .

- Do I believe my thoughts as though they are accurate representations of 'reality'?
- When I make attributions about motives, do I tend to give my partner the benefit of the doubt or do I assume the worst?
- Am I as good at making excuses for my partner as I am at doing so for myself?

THINGS TO DO

- Practise being aware of your thinking rather than letting your thoughts push you around. Remember to be non-judgemental as you notice your thoughts and as you learn more about them.
- Learn to differentiate 'first arrows', which cause you pain, from 'second arrows', which cause unnecessary suffering.
- Let go of beliefs that have been disproved, such as:
  —Conflict is bad.
  —We are the only couple with problems.
  —Partners cannot change.
  —Men and women come from different planets.
  —People are better off single.

CHAPTER 4

battling negativity

INTERMITTENTLY, I EXPERIENCE A PATCH of insomnia. If it goes on for too long I end up dragging myself through the day, battling a head cold, or the latest bug, and talking to family members through gritted teeth. Problems seem immense, permanent and impossible to resolve. Recently, I found myself enduring one of those days in which you feel tired and desperate for bedtime. In a dire physical state, I found myself ruminating over my latest spat with Tomek, which was about leisure time and who had more of it.

Rumination is a dangerous activity on one of these below par days. The negative feelings, such as anger and self-pity, can snowball until they assume a dangerous form. I was fortunate that I still had enough mindfulness and self-awareness to avoid inflicting a full-scale assault on Tomek when he arrived home, but I was still unstable enough to raise the sensitive topic. Fortunately, he was in a sound enough mood to make some conciliatory efforts and defer discussing the topic to a later date. That was lucky. If he had not been in good spirits, we might have had a major battle to navigate. And all for nothing.

You see, I slept about nine hours that night and when I woke up I felt restored and full of energy and optimism. I wondered what on earth I was so upset about the day before. I felt nothing but gratitude towards Tomek who had handled my comments in a way that defused the situation. I acknowledged that he had recently been making considerable efforts to ensure we both enjoyed some leisure time. In fact, I had to admit that he had been making an effort in many ways and that this made me feel quite warm towards him. Yet on the previous day, I saw none of these positives. The previous day, my life with Tomek had looked like a long road of never-ending drudgery, inequity and emotional neglect.

I pondered, if I can feel this way after a few bad nights of sleep, what would happen to the marriage if I was suffering an extended period of insomnia or illness? For all I know, menopause a few years down the track would bring exactly these challenges. I needed to think of some ways to protect myself.

My eldest son, Zac, is probably the happiest person I have ever known, yet sometimes at around bedtime he can become worried that some kind of minor disaster will befall him: he might fail a school test, he might not get picked for the team he wants to join, he might pick the wrong subject at school. While we might spend a little time talking through how realistic his fears are, I can usually make him smile by saying, 'Looks like you have late-night brain again'. Zac nods and appears to realise that an uncontrollable force influences his thoughts, namely, the time of day. He has learnt to take these late-night thoughts with a grain of salt. While he might not be able to block them out completely, he can still tune out, or treat them like an annoying television show, the content of which he is free to ignore. On such nights he might meditate himself to sleep, focusing on his breath or a body scan, relaxing his muscles from his toes, moving gradually to his face.

By using the Buddhist technique of labelling his thoughts—in this case, 'late-night brain'—he is less likely to become caught in them, lost in them, pushed around by them. I realised that I too should have been doing this on my bad day: labelling my ruminative processes 'exhaustion brain', and refusing to identify with all the melodramatic cognitions. It is, of course, terribly difficult to bring conscious awareness to our thinking when we are tired, ill or physically uncomfortable over an extended period. That's why repeatedly applying a label such as 'exhaustion brain' or 'late-night brain' can be so valuable: it doesn't take much effort and it protects us from the vortex of negativity.

I did find it helpful during that exhausted day to check in with my body and feel the tiredness, to be aware of the precise sensations in my body that go with being tired. This helped me to at least spare the children from my crankiness. When we fail to acknowledge our fatigue, or our dark mood, and the effect it has on our body, we can end up believing that our children, partner and whole life is incredibly irritating and overlook the fact that, in our current state, we are just incredibly irritable.

But the irritability will pass. Always does. And we needn't punish ourselves for it—it was just another passing state, not 'who I am'. When we are in a dark mood, our thoughts are not our friends. They are not on our side. They are rarely helpful. They could force us into damaging conflicts with our partner. Best give them the cold shoulder.

POSITIVE THINKING—NO SACRED COW

Several close friends have agreed with me when I have confided that, of all life's problems, marital rough patches feel the most destabilising to my emotional well-being. The sheer intensity of the anger, disappointment or sadness can, at times, completely overwhelm our capacity for mindfulness. And the relief of resolving a disagreement can be immense. While some friends have admitted to weeks of hostility, my preferred approach is to bring matters to a head for as swift a resolution as possible. This can be a highly emotional path for me to tread but I am not designed for long periods of tension.

So, how can we cope with the emotional maelstrom brought about by relationship tensions? As I was growing up, many of the adults around me encouraged me to adopt Pollyanna as my role model, the fictional character who always saw the bright side no matter what happened. Pollyanna never inspired me. I found her annoying. So it was with some relief that I heard the Buddha's First Noble Truth, that there is suffering, and that unsatisfactoriness, due to impermanence, is one of the 'marks of existence', a part of every phenomenon. This struck me as a far more realistic starting point on which to build a philosophy of life.

When we think of the times we have felt really down and tried to discuss our problems with a friend, we may have felt irritated (I know I have) if our friend's response was simply to remind us of the bright side. The reason we felt irritated was that our friend, usually despite the best of intentions, did not acknowledge our pain. They did not allow it to exist. We felt we had a right to our feelings but our confidante only tried to talk us out of them. Of course, there are times when some positive reassurance is all we need to feel better, but when we feel strongly affected by negative emotions caused by difficult issues, we probably want the listener to acknowledge our feelings and our right to feel them. This is why counsellors are trained to 'reflect feelings' by saying things like: 'I'm hearing that her actions caused a lot of anger for you,' or, 'That's a really hard situation. I think most people would feel as overwhelmed as you do.'

If our only tool to deal with our problems is positive thinking, then we treat ourselves the same way as the friend who insists on the bright side, and refuse to allow ourselves to feel perfectly natural emotions. That's why Buddhist teachers instruct us to 'just *be* with your anger', 'just *be* with your sadness', or with your exhaustion, your anxiety or your stress. No resistance. No struggle. No suppression. Make room for the emotion. Allow it to exist. Be curious, perhaps asking, *What is this?* Observe how the emotion feels in your body. Notice too how awareness of it diminishes its intensity.

Buddhist teachings are not about positive thinking but about increasing our capacity to see clearly and accurately so that we can respond to as close an approximation of reality as we can.

A ROLE FOR POSITIVE THINKING?

Although positive thinking is no sacred cow, when it comes to our relationship with our partners, it is easy to fall into a rut of negative thinking where all we see is their faults and the ways that they disappoint, if not infuriate, us. With the human bias for negativity, we need to ensure our critical thoughts do not swamp any grateful thoughts about our partner. So it is not a case of imposing 'positive thinking' over the top of bad situations but rather, in an effort to be more objective, trying to also remember the positive qualities of our partners.

A few years ago Tomek and I were engaged in some major battle, the cause of which I no longer remember. We had reached an impasse and were completely stuck, equally displeased with each other. In a random act of utter spontaneity, I grabbed a piece of paper and wrote out a list of the ten qualities I liked most about him and passed it to him, wordlessly. His face broke into a smile as he read it and the tension in the air dissolved. He gave me a hug and we both decided to let go of our negativity and be friends again. Just like that. Not that writing such a list will solve every argument but sometimes we need to force ourselves to remember the information beyond the negativity bias.

Writing a list of the ways your partner contributes to the household, or the qualities that you appreciate, is a worthwhile task in times of peace as well. If we become too fixated on all the ways our partner lets us down—and let's be honest, we often get fixated—we deny ourselves enjoyment from the ways our partner enhances our life. Given the force of the negativity bias, it is worth putting our list in a safe place for regular reference.

A friend of mine, Andrea, has a natural ability to focus on the positive. Her marriage can at times seem like a replica of mine: Andrea and I struggle with the same issues, seem to be similar personality types to each other, and are both married to similar types of men. Throughout the more challenging years, however, when the children were young, she always seemed happier than me in her marriage. The reasons would of course be too complex to psychoanalyse, but I did notice one glaring difference in our relationships. In a social context, Andrea and her husband Wayne never stopped promoting each other. She would proudly tell all assembled about her husband's achievements as a marathon runner, how much he made her laugh, what a good judge of character he was, even how much she liked the shape of his bum. He would compliment her cooking, boast about the size of her vocabulary, and inform us of her mastery of new technologies. They often created conversational openings for each other, 'Andrea, tell them about the time . . .'

Andrea and Wayne behaved like publicists for each other, tirelessly promoting, whereas Tomek and I rarely mentioned each other. I have noticed other friends and acquaintances engage in small plugs for their partner's qualities and I find it a beautiful, heartwarming gesture. Given that humiliating our partner in a social situation is often reported as one of the worst betrayals a partner can commit, how powerful it must be to do the opposite.

•

I must say, over the years, I have made peace with Pollyanna. While positive thinking can go too far and turn into denial, maybe it has its place. The Buddha, while focusing on the benefits of bare attention, was by no means inflexible about how we cope with unskilful or unhelpful thoughts that lead to painful results. This quotation from the Buddha suggests a place for positive thinking:

If some unskilled thoughts associated with desire, aversion or confusion arise and disturb the mind, you should attend instead to another characteristic which is associated with what is skilled . . . It is like a skilled carpenter who can knock out a large peg with a small peg.

Among other advice to help his followers deal with unskilled thoughts, he suggested we:

- consider the painful results of unskilled thoughts
- bring about forgetfulness and lack of attention to unskilled thoughts
- consider alternative, 'easier' thoughts
- use our willpower to overcome the unskilled thoughts.

The Buddha presents these ideas as options, knowing that it depends on the situation which one will work best. Of course, the task of catching ourselves, realising that we are lost in unhelpful thoughts, can be the greatest challenge of all. That's why practising mindfulness of thoughts as often as possible is so worthwhile.

Sometimes favouring positive thoughts over negative ones is brave and heroic, as in the case of one man whose biography I wrote. Hamish suffered two strokes early in his retirement, which put him in a wheelchair and introduced many difficulties into his life. Yet he always spoke to me about how much he valued positive thinking, noticing all his blessings, as a way of coping with his situation. Admittedly, his positive approach only developed after he had worked his way through more difficult emotions, including a strong desire to end it all. I found his efforts to savour the blessings admirable, not to mention considerate of his wife and carer, Nina.

Within our relationships, positive thinking is perhaps something many of us would love our partner to practise more. None of us want to hear a stream of negativity from our partner for too long. We all have a responsibility to add a little cheer to the atmosphere of our household rather than drag everybody down, expressing all our negative thoughts day after day.

•

In January 2013 I treated myself to an afternoon at Sydney Opera House watching an interview with Elizabeth Gilbert, the author of *Eat, Pray, Love*. (I know, I know, the movie was terrible . . .) I had enjoyed the humour, insight and quality of writing in all her books and found her delightful in person too: funny, gracious, loving, grounded. At one point, the interviewer asked Elizabeth what had been the single best thing that happened to her as a result of the whole *Eat, Pray, Love* journey. I leant forward to hear her answer, mentally flicking through the possibilities. *Meeting the man she would marry? The feeling of validation that comes with success? Making a fortune? Having her life turned into a movie? Meeting Javier Bardem? Appearing on Oprah?*

But no.

Her answer was simply 'the four months in India'. There, through meditation and reflection, she discovered the helpful voice in her mind, which she described as the mother of all the 'insane children', all the 'anxious orphans' that chatter in her head. She described the newfound voice as 'the mum in the mini-van', who calmly says, 'Shhhh, quieten down, Mummy's driving'. Now, Elizabeth doesn't have children so has no way of knowing what mothers in mini-vans really sound like, but I appreciate her point. She discovered a higher voice that could calm the crazier ones, the voice that knew that thoughts are only thoughts, not truths.

THINGS TO CONTEMPLATE . . .

- Do you force yourself to be Pollyanna-positive at times when you need to make compassionate space for visits from negative emotions?
- Do you remind yourself often of your partner's positive qualities and contributions?

THINGS TO DO

- Avoid ruminating, particularly when you feel exhausted. Try to recognise catastrophic thoughts.
- Label your thoughts when you feel tired—'late-night brain' or 'exhaustion brain'—as a reminder that your thoughts are trouble-makers at such times.
- When tired, tune in to the sensations of the body. Surrender to them rather than waste energy resisting them.
- Keep a list of positive qualities or reasons to feel grateful towards your partner. Remember to revisit your list from time to time.
- Speak highly of your partner on social occasions. Never put them down in front of others.
- Develop tolerance for unpleasant emotions through the practice of *being with* them, or allowing space for them, rather than blocking or suppressing them. They are all just temporary visitors. Be curious about them.

- Keep positive thinking as part of your toolkit but realise that the Buddha offered several options for dealing with unhelpful thoughts.
- Admit that noticing the positives, or being upbeat, as often as possible is a good influence on the atmosphere of your household.

CHAPTER 5

anger

The one who offends another
After being offended by him,
Harms himself and harms the other.
When you feel hurt
But do not hurt the other,
You are truly victorious.
Your practice and your victory benefit both of you.
When you understand the roots of anger in yourself
And in the other,
Your mind will enjoy true peace, joy and lightness.
You become the doctor who heals himself and heals the other.
If you don't understand,
You will think not getting angry to be the act of a fool.

The Buddha

IMAGINE PICKING UP A book about relationships and reading advice like this:

- If you really want your message to sink in, raise your voice a few decibels.
- Talking through gritted teeth helps to convey how strongly you feel and should achieve your goals.
- Expressing contempt is a powerful tool.
- An angry look can work a treat.
- Give sulking a try.

It is laughable to think we would ever find such a book. Yet these methods of addressing relationship issues are ones we often resort to. We may also have noticed that these methods force both members of a couple into self-defence mode, where both are incapable of feeling any sympathy for their partner's point of view—if they hear it at all. It is not so much that these methods do not achieve results. As with parenting, anger can certainly produce compliance. It is just that we have to pay for compliance with the precise things we all want most from a relationship: affection, goodwill and a pleasant emotional climate. Another price we pay for angry outbursts is in terms of information. One mother describes such a situation involving her son Jack:

> Yesterday I went to a parent–teacher interview about Jack but I've decided not to discuss that conversation with my husband. Jack is not fulfilling his potential at school—he just wants to put in a minimum effort and have fun. If I told my husband he would just yell at Jack and call him lazy and Jack would cry and feel ashamed. I feel like my husband's approach to the problem just makes Jack more sneaky—he tends to hide from us any poor results and avoid talking about any failures. I don't want my son to develop exam anxiety, nor do I want him to study just to please his parents. He's only ten, after all.

Yes, if our partner has a temper, we can feel obliged to withhold all sorts of information in order to keep the peace. Sadly, the more information we have to withhold, the less open and authentic our relationship can be.

Anger tends to be accompanied by delusion. It stops us from thinking clearly, which is why it can bring us to take rash action, or say hurtful things we later regret. It gives us tunnel vision, blinding us to other options of responding. It can make our thinking fixated and repetitive, enslaving us. It fails to see impermanence, causes, conditions and complexity as it reduces people and events to stereotypes. We start to see people in fixed, inflexible ways.

Some psychology literature explains that when we make sacrifices for a partner, be it cooking dinner or moving cities, we do so either to gain a reward or avoid a cost. When someone feels he must 'walk on eggshells' around a temperamental partner, his motivation is to avoid complaints rather than enjoy rewards. How superior it would be for him to make those same sacrifices, in the hope of rewards. The rewards might include a feeling of working as a team in the interests of the household, maintenance of a strong, committed partnership or simple appreciation. When too many of our interactions with our partner are motivated by a need to avoid the unpleasant, rather than a desire to reinforce the positives, relationship quality declines and the relationship is more vulnerable to dissolution.[1]

DON'T FEEL GUILTY

Those of us who come from a Judeo–Christian background might note the Buddha's views on anger and decide that anger is a sin and something to feel guilty about. We might feel like a 'bad person', a failure, after we lose our temper. That is to say we take it very personally, believing the anger is a manifestation of who we are, perhaps all we are. Yet we are so much more than this temporary emotion that arises due to a stream of causes and conditions. These might include stress, fatigue, our habitual interpretations of events, family background, or cultural or gender-based expectations around dealing with stress. So self-compassion would be a more logical response to our anger than guilt and shame.

The arising of angry feelings, given all the causes and conditions, may be understandable, even quite reasonable. That said, we are still responsible for how we deal with angry feelings once they have arisen. What we can do is gradually learn to manage the anger in a constructive way, to relate to it in new ways, with ever increasing awareness. Observing the anger, being there for it—perhaps labelling it, *Anger is here now*—and accepting its presence helps us to refrain from adding more emotions such as guilt, disappointment in ourselves, or more anger.

DON'T CHASE THE ARSONIST

Despite all the pitfalls of expressing anger unskilfully, only last weekend I initiated an angry exchange with my husband. An inequity had been frustrating me but, with our children in the vicinity, I had been reluctant to address it. Finally, I asked Tomek to come upstairs for a quick word where I socked him with it. Conscious of little listening ears, trying to keep my voice down, I delivered my complaint in a quiet voice but through gritted teeth. I imagine my face looked quite angry.

To my amazement he did not say, 'Yeah, you've got a point. I will behave differently from now on.'

No. He lashed back at me and within a minute had left the room in disgust. Being me, I was plunged into a state of anxiety and distress.

Two hours later Tomek and I were at a fortieth birthday party, mingling among all the happy couples. How carefree they looked, out on the dance floor, so unaware of the tension behind our party faces.

The next day, Sunday, Tomek was out all day at the car-racing track and I picked up a book entitled, simply, *Anger*. The author, Vietnamese Zen teacher Thich Nhat Hanh, advised me to say to my 'beloved': 'Darling, I am angry. I suffer. I am doing my best. Please help me.'

As lovely as this sounds, this is not really our style of communication. We did manage to do a quick patch-up job before work on Monday morning though. Still, I had ruined my weekend. What had possessed me to address the issue so unskilfully?

Thich Nhat Hanh made this accurate diagnosis of my weekend: 'The fact is that when you make the other suffer, he will try to find relief by making you suffer more . . . If your house is on fire, the most urgent thing to do is to go back and try to put out the fire, not to run after the person you believe to be the arsonist.'[2] Thich Nhat Hanh believes that we should not act while our anger is at a peak but turn inwards first to take care of the anger. Fire is an excellent metaphor for the topic of anger: we need to be very careful to contain its spread and its potential for harm. We can address the issue with the arsonist when we have calmed down. A spot of mindful breathing can ease the way. This need not be in a spirit of suppression but with awareness that there is a higher way available to deal with the feelings. Even non-Buddhists advise counting to ten.

Thich Nhat Hanh said that we don't need punishment for our relationship problems, we need compassion and help. I took him at his word and sought help. I emailed a Buddhist psychologist friend asking if she could put me in touch with a Buddhist couples therapist.

'Geoff Dawson' came her reply. Not only was Geoff a Buddhist psychologist and couples therapist, he was also the teacher of the Ordinary Mind Zen School established by the late Charlotte Joko Beck, a highly respected Zen teacher from the United States. Geoff had been practising Buddhism since 1975, including a stint in a Japanese monastery. I decided Geoff would be just the professional to help me disentangle some of my karmic knots. I was off to couples counselling.

Ironically, alone.

SO ANGRY I COULD JUST . . .

Some time in my twenties, a friend confided in me: 'My father was a harsh man and I think I have internalised a part of him in my own personality. I certainly have a cruel streak—I call it my inner bully.'

'Really?' I asked, gobsmacked. 'But you seem too nice to have any bully in you.'

'Oh, I do,' she assured me, with all the conviction of someone who has paid for a lot of therapy. We remained friends but I always felt a little wary around her, worried I might someday provoke her inner bully.

It took me years to discover, no doubt helped by practising mindfulness of my thoughts, that I have an inner bully of my own. I am supposed to be a Buddhist practitioner, cultivating compassion and kindness. Yet I have been amazed at how vindictive and cruel some of my thoughts can be when I feel angry or even just irritated. My imagination can be a tough neighbourhood at times. Thankfully, I have enough self-control to never (well, rarely) act on these thoughts, but it horrifies me to notice them arise.

I decided to tell Geoff, my new Buddhist couples therapist, about my inner bully, although I did fear he might think less of me as a Buddhist practitioner and an author of Buddhist books.

'Hmm, yeah,' said Geoff, sounding underwhelmed. 'I've got an inner bully too. Lots of the people in my Zen group talk about their inner bullies. I think knowledge of the inner bully is something that comes with Buddhist practice. You become aware of any aggression, hatred, hostility that you may have swept under the carpet in the past. But with practice, instead of taking it out on someone, you notice it and are able to manage it.'

'Not everyone has one though,' I added. 'I know people—some people who are quite close to me—who don't seem to have any bully in their nature.'

'No,' Geoff concurred. 'But often something else will be happening with those people, like they turn the hostility against themselves. They are more likely to be depressed, for example.'

This did seem to be the case for the two people I had in mind.

I was most relieved to know that someone like Geoff, an actual Zen teacher, had an inner bully. It reminded me of a favourite quotation by prisoner of the Soviet gulags, Aleksandr Solzhenitsyn. His words have comforted me in times of guilt after my inner bully has surfaced: 'If only there were evil people somewhere insidiously committing evil deeds, and it were necessary only to separate them from the rest of us and destroy them. But the line dividing good and evil cuts through the heart of every human being.'3

My conversation with Geoff made me wonder what happens to people who have no means of making sense of their inner bully. I speculated that in many cases they must feel terribly guilty, possibly to the point of self-loathing, possibly perceiving themselves as a social fraud or freak. Then there would be others happy to convert the inner bully into an outer bully and inflict their cruelty on others.

Our work is not to silence the bully, however. Solzhenitsyn continues: 'And who is willing to destroy a piece of his own heart?' As Geoff said, rather than suppress the bully we can notice it and manage it. I asked Geoff what might be involved in 'managing' it.

'Often,' he began, 'when our response to others feels hostile, we only notice anger. If we sit with the feeling and really investigate it though, behind the self-righteousness we often find fear, shame or insecurity. Of course, it takes a lot of honesty and humility to admit this to ourselves but if we can get in touch with that insecurity we find the angry response softens.'

I considered my own inner bully and conceded that it was in fact a panic merchant, desperate to cover up my own perceived weaknesses, especially feelings of worthlessness, any sense of failure, or fears of being unlovable. A most convenient cover-up, the inner bully.

Geoff also had some good news for me: 'If we don't acknowledge our inner bully we risk becoming one of those people you find in spiritual communities who do not integrate the angry, or less attractive parts of themselves. We can be so intent on being a nice, spiritual person that we end up denying a large part of our experience rather than working with it.'

One advantage of becoming more familiar with our inner bully is that we become more understanding towards people who are yet to bring the bullying aspects of their nature under control. As we watch them act out, we might even say to ourselves, 'That's just like me'. We can acknowledge that they too may be acting from a place of fear with an exaggerated sense of the self and the need to defend it.

I decided to make some more appointments with Geoff.

DON'T YOU HAVE TO LET IT OUT?

A great deal of the language we use around anger suggests it is a force that builds up and must be released: we must 'vent', 'let it out', 'let off steam'. We tell each other, 'Don't bottle it up or you'll explode'. Both Aristotle and Freud warned against the building up of negative emotions, which might eventually result in hysteria. The modern scientific community is in no doubt, however, that venting our anger is not the way to deal with it. Venting has, in fact, been found to increase hostile feelings, aggressive tendencies and violence. Whereas in the past, psychologists might have advised us to take our anger out on a punching bag, hit a tree with a stick or yell at someone, this is now antiquated thinking. As one scientific journal put it: 'Because venting is an aggressive activity, it keeps the anger alive by stimulating physiological arousal, aggressive thoughts, angry feelings, and aggressive impulses.'[4]

So why have humans clung to the idea that they need to vent their anger? The article continues: 'The fact that anger does eventually dissipate with time, regardless of what people do, might also foster the illusion that venting works. What people fail to realize is that the anger would have dissipated had they not vented.'

If a discussion with our partner is becoming too heated, a wise thing to do might be to call an adjournment. Agree to return to the issue at a later point when we can speak more calmly. This might take considerable self-discipline when we are in full flight, but it can also avoid harm to the relationship through hurtful comments. Such an adjournment is also more likely to lead to a peaceful resolution than if we continually attack each other and the focus of the discussion remains on self-defence.

I know Buddhists who have made a vow to abandon all angry exchanges. They may fail in their vow again and again but they can always forgive themselves and renew their vow. Such a vow comes from an understanding that expressing raw anger with an emotional attack on another is likely to be harmful.

To quote the Buddha:

Having slain anger, one sleeps soundly;
Having slain anger, one does not sorrow.
The killing of anger, O radiant being,
With its poisoned root and honeyed tip:
This is the killing that the noble ones praise.
For having slain that, one does not sorrow.

If vowing to abandon anger feels too ambitious for you, take heart. Relationship guru John Gottman found that anger alone did not predict divorce or separation. In his extensive and world-renowned studies, plenty of couples who experienced, and expressed, anger managed to stay together. What predicted divorce was how negative the expression of anger was: if the anger was expressed with criticism, contempt or defensiveness, then divorce was far more likely.[5]

RESPONDING TO OUR ANGER

None of this is to say that we should ignore, deny or suppress anger. Anger exists because throughout human history it has been useful in ensuring our survival: it has led us to defend ourselves in moments of danger. Even in modern times, anger is useful if it motivates us to confront injustice. If we can do so without causing harm to others, and with compassion for our opponent, then we are more effective. The natural arising of anger is not the problem. Rather, the problem is our failure to be aware of the arising of anger and manage it. This leads to a habit-driven conversion of anger into regrettable behaviour (read snapping, sniping, yelling, blaming).

So if venting is counterproductive, we need to consider other options. One is to shift our perspective regarding our partner's offence. As we discussed in the last chapter, we can examine our interpretation of the offence in question: does our interpretation enhance the relationship or maintain distress? Have we given our partner the benefit of the doubt? Additionally, we can consider how we ourselves have contributed to the problem including whether we have remembered compassion for our partner's *dukkha*, their suffering, as well as our own. We can challenge our false sense of separation, remember our interdependence or oneness, and remember that our exaggerated sense of 'self and other' is an illusion. Given that anger causes tunnel vision, we can also consider how our anger has blinded us to other aspects of the problem.

What intrigues me about my own experiences of anger is that even though I realise, on a rational level, that anger is just an impermanent mind state, it feels so permanent at the time. We fuel this impression by telling ourselves, *I* always *have to put up with this; it's been going on for so long; what if it continues forever?* It is reassuring to remind ourselves that this highly unpleasant emotion, like any emotion, will not linger long.

MINDFULNESS OF THE BODY

While the benefits of mindful breathing are widely recognised, the Buddha also spoke of mindfulness of the body. If we can bring our awareness to the body in the present moment, we can locate the anger. We may find tension in our face or shoulders, butterflies in the stomach, clenching of our fists, tightening of the jaw. If we guide our attention to these bodily sensations, we become less caught up in ruminating thoughts. With the power of mere attention, we feel the easing of tension in our bodies, and we grow calmer. We may notice our breath deepen and slow down without even forcing it to. Body awareness will always reduce the intensity of our anger.

For me, mindfulness has meant noticing how often I am in automatic-pilot mode when interacting with Tomek, caught up in habitual, mindless ways of thinking and interacting. To be honest, I find the partner relationship the hardest one to approach mindfully. For some reason, I find it easier to be mindful of my interactions with strangers, acquaintances, my friends and my children. Yet this is all the more reason for me to keep trying to bring awareness to the relationship I take most for granted.

Then again, what if the intensity of our feelings makes mindfulness, makes turning inward, feel impossible? Buddhist friend Carlos tells me he struggles with anger, such as overreacting to children arguing, to their resisting his requests to tidy up, and to marital quibbling.

He finds it easier to direct his mindfulness on what is 'outward' than inward:

> Sometimes my anger can feel too overwhelming and I feel power-less to deal with it or to be mindful. I've learnt that physical activity and a change of scene helps me change my perspective and reduces the intensity of my anger. Rather than pay attention to my thoughts or my body sensations, I find it easier to practise awareness of my surroundings. I am lucky that my wife tends to be home to stay with our young children if I need to take a ten-minute walk around the block to collect myself. She encourages me to do this, knowing it is better than the alternative of a shouting match. Taking a mindful walk is an opportunity to tune into my senses as I pay attention to the sights, the sounds, the smells I come across. I notice thoughts arise and let them go, returning to the sensory details of the present moment. When I walk in the door again I feel as though I have recharged my batteries and I'm capable of being with my family in a calmer way.

ACCEPTING AN OPPORTUNITY TO LEARN AND GROW

My friend Robin from my Buddhist group is a couples psychotherapist who teaches mindfulness to her clients.

> When I first started practising Buddhist teachings, before I really understood them, I was not really aware of my anger or that I even experienced hatred. I think the word for this is 'over-socialised'—such emotions were not socially acceptable in my world. I believed then that anger and hatred were feelings you chose to have and that you could control and eliminate

them if you wished. This approach eventually backfired as I ended up somatising negative feelings like anger, sadness and fear. In other words, my body expressed my anger on a subconscious level through rheumatism, swollen painful joints and chronic tiredness.

As my meditation practice advanced, along with my studies in counselling and psychotherapy, I eventually gave myself permission to accept that negative feelings and emotions are inevitable and to care for them like I would a child, a suffering friend, or a visiting guest: that is, with compassion and kindness. That's what I do with the couples who see me. I encourage couples to relate with loving kindness and acceptance of the negative feelings that arise in their relationship for these are opportunities for growth, for increased understanding and compassion, and for a richer, more meaningful life together.

Robin has transformed her aversion to negative feelings into an acceptance of them and even an 'embracing' of them. She argues we need to accept that suffering will inevitably visit us, in the form of anger or critical thoughts, so we may as well accept these feelings and welcome them. If we push them away we might end up finding a deadness and boredom setting in to our lives and relationships—the beginnings of emotional divorce or even a cold war.

As Robin says, in order to live life fully we need to appreciate and embrace both the agony and ecstasy of daily life in all its wonder. We need to daily celebrate, and mourn, our life together. (For myself, I have to say that I am a long way from being capable of welcoming negative emotions or embracing agony while in the thick of it. I can't even imagine how that works . . . Still, some Buddhists, most often from the visionary Tibetan tradition, speak in these terms. Maybe in retrospect, after the intensity of an incident has passed, it is possible for me to embrace the suffering, when I can see how it has made me more compassionate or taught me something I needed to learn.)

Robin continues, speaking about her clients:

> With acceptance of anger and other negative feelings comes increased insight into suffering and into our needs, such as for safety, belonging, acceptance, or love. With acceptance of suffering—the inevitability of conflict and negative feelings—couples are better equipped to find more creative solutions to their issues than if they only rely on unproductive arguing. For instance, if my partner accepts my anger while giving me a hug, or if I am held when angry, a feeling of deep healing can occur.

Personally, I wouldn't want to be hugged in a moment of anger (it might even be dangerous). Maybe later on. We're all different though and our task is to find out what works in comforting our own partners. As Robin suggests, accepting the existence, and inevitability, of negative feelings in ourselves and our partner, is a sound first step.

RAIN

Jack Kornfield, Buddhist teacher and one of the leaders in introducing Buddhist practice to the West, has developed a useful acronym that captures the Buddhist response to negative emotions: RAIN. First, we need to Recognise that anger has arisen, acknowledge its presence rather than responding with denial, numbing, alcohol or blame. Next, we need to Accept the presence of the emotion; we need to allow it to exist rather than suppressing it for being unpleasant or unflattering to our sense of self. Thirdly, we Investigate the emotion, applying genuine curiosity, perhaps even asking, *What is this?* We locate the experience of the emotion in the body, the tensions and contractions in our muscles. We notice the thoughts that fuel the emotion. We open ourselves to the feeling tone, knowing it is impermanent. Finally, we Non-identify with the emotion. That is, we refuse to see it as who we are. We might borrow the words of the Buddha: 'I am not this, this is not me, this is not myself.' The emotion is something everyone experiences and not something special about me.

Recognise, Accept, Investigate, Non-identify.[6]

No need to punish

We sometimes find ourselves clinging to a state of anger because we believe we need to punish our partner. We believe our partner has made us suffer and must not be allowed to walk free. Forgetting that our partner cannot read our minds, we think that holding onto our anger will teach them a lesson. With this mindset, we tend to punish ourselves the most by denying our minds freedom from anger. Moreover, that mindset is unnecessary, for karma means that we will reap what we sow. The Buddha said:

> Speak or act with an impure mind
> And trouble will follow you
> As the wheel follows the ox that draws the cart . . .
> Speak or act with a pure mind
> And happiness will follow you
> As your shadow, unshakable.

The law of karma applies as much to our partner as to ourselves. There is no need for anyone to play God: it's all taken care of. Many people, including many Buddhists all over the world, misinterpret karma as being about some supernatural deliverance of divine retribution for misdeeds—which is quite a spooky interpretation. The literal translation of the sanskrit word 'karma' is simply 'action'. Every act we engage in has an intention behind it, and in Buddhism it is the intention that is critical to our karma. If we act with bad intentions, we are likely to experience unpleasant results at some point down the road. The best example of these unpleasant results is that every time we act with bad intentions we increase the likelihood we will do so again because every act creates seeds in our minds that will sprout given the appropriate conditions. In neuroscience, the buzzword is 'plasticity', whereby the more we activate a particular neural pathway, the stronger it becomes and the more likely it is that we will reactivate it again in the future. We end up with some well-worn pathways in our brains because those are the pathways we have reinforced.

Given that our partner will surely suffer, in some way, following any misbehaviour, we might even feel compassion for them.

THINGS TO CONTEMPLATE . . .

- What are some of the costs of anger in my household? Withholding of information? White lies? Less goodwill?
- Are my actions in relation to my partner motivated by cost-avoiding or reward-seeking? And which of these most motivates my partner's actions?
- Do I habitually interpret my partner's behaviours in ways that enhance the relationship or ones that cause me distress?
- Do I feel that anger is necessary in order to punish my partner? If so, could I let go of my need to punish and replace it with compassion for a partner who might have some bad karma coming their way?

THINGS TO DO

- Accept the presence of anger, perhaps labelling it, *Anger is here now*. Acceptance helps us to avoid adding to the anger emotions such as guilt, disappointment in ourselves, or more anger.
- Do not act, or speak, when anger is at its peak. Calm down, perhaps by using mindfulness of the breath or body, before taking action.
- Don't feel guilty or shocked to discover you have an inner bully. Just manage it skilfully.
- Don't see your partner, or yourself, as 'good' or 'bad' for we are all a complex mix of both.
- Recognise and become familiar with the fear that underlies anger.
- Don't fall for the myth of 'venting'.
- Remind yourself that anger is impermanent, even though it doesn't feel like it at the time.
- Tune into the sensations of the body in times of anger as a way to detach from the thinking, ruminating mind and return to the present moment.
- Care for yourself when angry, as you would a house guest or a distressed child.
- Recognise the opportunities for learning and growth that can accompany episodes of anger, especially learning about each other's needs.
- Consider a role for nature, or gentle exercise, in the process of calming down.
- Practise RAIN: Recognise, Accept, Investigate and Non-identify with anger.

CHAPTER 6

housework

IN THE FIRST DRAFT of this book I included the topic of housework in the chapter on anger as the two go together for many couples. Such a bone of contention in so many relationships, housework eventually warranted a chapter of its own. With a strong commitment to feminist principles I was never going to be one of those women who settled for a raw deal on the division of housework. Alas, I now somehow find myself with so little bargaining power, and no hope of winning an argument with a man whose financial contribution to the household and hours spent at the office so outdo my own.

Admittedly, I am probably among the more fortunate partners. As a neat type, Tomek generates no mess. He cooks one meal most weeks, does an occasional laundry load, the odd supermarket run and a little outdoor work. It's just that there is so much more than this to the grind of keeping house. So much of the work is invisible even to ourselves—cleaning bins, removing rotting banana from school bags, clearing toast crumbs, cleaning the microwave—such that you can scratch your head in wonder, 'What did I actually do all afternoon?' I do concede that given the pressures Tomek faces at work, along with the proportion of the household income he earns, that I need to do somewhat more than 50 per cent of the housework. It's a matter of negotiating just what that proportion should be.

Another large problem for me is a perceptual one, whereby Tomek loads the dishwasher maybe once a fortnight and suddenly complains he 'always' loads the dishwasher. It's hard to feel appreciated when you struggle even to win the argument of who is doing what. In his defence, it is apparently quite normal to overestimate the number of hours we contribute to housework. Researchers explain that it is easier to remember a task we actively engaged in, and which took our time, than to remember all the times we overlooked a job left undone.[1]

I decided to run the whole housework conundrum by Geoff at one of our sessions.

'How on earth,' I began, 'can you practise Buddhist non-attachment around housework? How do you not become upset, furious even, if you feel ripped off about how much you have to do compared to your partner? I don't believe the Buddhist antidote is to become a doormat and—'

'Oh no,' cried Geoff. 'If you feel the division is unfair you have to address that. You have to be assertive. This issue comes up a lot with the couples I work with and what I find is that people seem to respond to the problem using one of two extremes: they either do the lion's share and become resentful or they confront their partner in an unskilful way, being hostile or aggressive. The question is not, in my mind, whether you address the issue but the way you address it.'

I had a flashback to a child psychologist addressing a group of parents at a seminar. He had said, 'If you have not had any success changing a situation with your current strategy, FIND A NEW ONE! I get so many parents telling me: "I've yelled at him twenty times about . . . whatever issue".' Likewise with our partners, if we have been addressing a problem such as housework in a way that does not achieve results we might need to think of a fresh strategy. What was that saying? The definition of insanity is doing the same thing over and over again and expecting a different result. Some of us, for example, opt for nagging as a way to address inequity in housework. (Reminds me of the book Marge was reading in one *Simpsons* episode, *Nagging your Way to Ecstasy*.)

Geoff was adamant that we continue to struggle for equity. 'I once asked myself, what would be the three characteristics I would most like for my Zen students to cultivate and I decided they were kindness, calmness and assertiveness.'

I tried to picture myself confronting the housework tensions in my home more kindly, calmly and assertively.

'I have to say though,' I challenged him, 'I've never heard the word *assertive* used in any Buddhist scripture.' This was perhaps an unfair comment. The word assertive, as used in modern times to describe behaviour that takes the middle road between passivity and aggression, has only been in common usage since the late 1970s.

'But if you meet any monks, or nuns, or highly experienced meditators, you do find they are assertive. They have a confidence that fuels their work.'

I had to concede that this was often the case. The Australian nun Robina Courtin from the Tibetan tradition sprang to mind. Recognising that righteous anger was making her 'crazy', Robina turned to Buddhist practice and tamed the anger that marked her former life as a self-described lesbian feminist separatist.

'I guess you could say,' I suggested, 'that behaving assertively shows compassion for yourself, which is definitely one of the aims of practice.'

'Confidence comes from humbleness,' Geoff threw in unexpectedly.

'What?' I asked, trying to process his words. 'How can that work?'

'The more we practise the teachings, the more we shed self-doubt, all the while increasing our understanding that this "self" we thought we had to protect, does not exist in the way we thought it did. Without so much self-doubt, and with a clearer view of the way things are, we increase our capacity to be assertive and confident.'

'So confidence comes from loosening our grip on that exaggerated sense of a self,' I tried to summarise.

'I gave a talk on this once,' said Geoff, warming to his topic. 'If you look at the word "humility", it comes from the Latin root "*humus*", which means ground. With practice we develop humility. We become more grounded, more down-to-earth, and when we walk on the ground we can't fall. This gives us confidence.'

UNDERSTANDING THE CAUSES AND CONDITIONS BEHIND HOUSEWORK INEQUITY

A friend of mine has consulted a couple of counsellors about her marriage but has not been satisfied with the result:

> Each time I've spoken to a counsellor I've explained the details of my marriage that drive me nuts and mostly it has been about unfairness. I feel like my husband gets away with so much more than I do whether we're talking about time for himself, housework, childcare or emotional support. But each counsellor I've seen has taken my side and agreed that my situation is unfair. This hasn't helped me because, given that my husband is not going to change overnight, what I really need is a way to handle my emotions as I continue living with unfairness. I don't need to be told I'm right when it comes to fairness. I already know that. What I want to know is how to live with this frustration.

It is so easy to demonise a partner who fails to do a fair share of housework and childcare. They do not play fair, therefore, they are bad, bad, bad. Buddhist teachings, however, encourage us to avoid perceiving anything in a vacuum and, rather, to see things as a result of their causes and conditions. This is the Buddha's teaching of *dependent arising*: everything is dependent on something else. Nothing exists on its own; nothing is independent. The Buddha said that to understand the teaching of dependent arising is to be enlightened, so there are many levels of understanding of this teaching.

I don't want to make excuses for partners who are not fair, nor let them off the hook, but it can help us to feel less hostile, less upset, if we consider some of the causes and some of the prevailing conditions around us, for any failure in our partner to take enough responsibility. I will do this with the help of Dr Joshua Coleman, author of *The Lazy Husband: How to get men to do more parenting and housework.*[2] He is a self-described 'reformed lazy husband' as well as a couples therapist, who seems to have developed genuine sympathy for the overworked wives of the world. To help us better understand the 'lazy husband' he offers several explanations for inequity in the division of childcare and housework. So instead of perceiving a partner as inherently bad, we see them as the result of a number of causes and conditions and this makes the whole issue feel less personal.

- Competence in parenting is more central to a woman's identity and self-esteem than it is to men's.
- Social expectations of housework and parenting demand more of women than of men so women are more motivated to meet these expectations and avoid harsh judgements from others. Poor performance in either area tends to reflect more badly on the woman than the man socially.
- Men are disproportionately respected for their status and earning power compared to their contribution to the family. They feel more of a need to compete with other men who are earning money and improving their status.
- Men look to the behaviour of other men, rather than to their wife, to consider what a fair contribution might be, and this reinforces inequity. They also look to their own fathers' contributions, and feel they have significantly improved on that.
- Females are encouraged, expected and rewarded, from a young age, to consider the feelings of others and look after others. Little girls at play also show more interest in taking turns, comforting others and playing fairly than little boys who play in ways that reinforce their sense of power.

Dr Coleman optimistically emphasises that all these forces are evolving in the right direction as society begins to expect more from men and men expect more from themselves.

In particular, engaging meaningfully with the role of father is becoming more central to the male identity, Coleman notes. A close friend of mine, Jenny, has grown-up children who have started having babies. Jenny has helped her daughter host barbecues and other gatherings for her daughter's new friends with babies. After each occasion she has reported back to me, 'Sarah! The fathers are changing nappies unasked and doting on their babies and toddlers—they're spending good stretches of time interacting with them.' She is impressed with both her son-in-law and her son, attentive fathers who appear to understand the importance of quality time with their new children. 'There's real hope for this new generation,' she enthuses.

While completely reforming a partner who doesn't pull their weight is beyond the scope of my book, Coleman's book offers different advice for different types of marriages. I checked with a friend, Viv, who recently read it, and she emailed back:

Hi Sarah

I really enjoyed reading that book and would like to read it again. Husband was quite offended by the title! The thing I really took away and am trying to implement is that you are more likely to get what you want if you frame things in a certain way, eg, be very grateful for something they've done and then ask for things in an affectionate tone. It can almost kill you but I do believe that it is very good advice and a positive method to get what you want. I am trying to remember to do this.

The feminist in me baulks at being 'very grateful' to my husband for doing housework. Doesn't that suggest that housework is women's work and women should appreciate any 'help' men 'generously' provide to us? Then again, if we want someone to repeat a behaviour, Psychology 101 taught us we need to reinforce that behaviour with a reward. I guess I have to keep asking myself that golden question: would you rather be right or happy?

JUST KEEP STRUGGLING

In her book *Wifework: What marriage really means for women,* Susan Maushart lists all the disappointing gender-based inequities of modern-day marriage before trying, in the final chapter, to come up with an approach for dealing with it all. She discourages wives from assigning blame, explaining that blaming feminism would be like 'blaming black unemployment on the abolition of slavery'. Blaming society would be like saying, 'I'm just following orders'. Blaming the individual we live with would also be counterproductive: 'Women who express their unhappiness with the wifely role through husband-bashing generally achieve very little anyway. They are dismissed as "attacking" or "controlling" and too often end up by accepting that their discontents are "their own problem".'[3]

Confronting our partners, Maushart continues, only seems to reinforce the cliché of women as the displeased grown-ups and men as 'cheeky little boys'. While there is no secret answer to the problem, she adds, 'Yet I am passionately convinced that we need to keep on struggling anyway. Who was it who said that lost causes are the only ones worth fighting for?' Her reason to continue the struggle: for the sake of our children who learn from what we model to them and who, these days, at least witness a better, albeit not yet equitable, model than we, their parents, witnessed. She has a point: I always wonder if my future daughter-in-laws will blame me, and the model I provided, if my sons grow up to be unfair about sharing the housework.

Bettina Arndt, however, sees the situation differently. In a fierce argument with Maushart on television show *Lateline* she accused Maushart of being disingenuous:

> If you really look at the research in that area it's very clear . . . couples are making a lot of decisions together. Women are taking other things into account when they assess whether it really matters how many nappies they change. If you look at the Australian data, if you add together the amount of unpaid work that men and women do there's about half an hour between them . . . Couples know that men do a whole lot of horrible things too.[4]

Arndt suggests there is the potential for women to feel less resentful if they consider the challenges and difficulties their partner faces.

For some women, accepting traditional gender roles on the grounds that their partner works hard too, spells the end of the whole problem and they are free to live with peace of mind. Many of us, for a million good reasons, cannot walk that path. I try to 'continue the struggle', as Susan Maushart puts it, in subtle ways, always mindful of my tone of voice. I might say, 'I'm feeling about due for a rest from cooking dinner . . .' (Instead of, 'For God's sake, could you give me a break from cooking!')

I also try to elicit appreciation, 'Did you notice that dirty cupboard is now completely clean?' (Instead of 'Thanks for ignoring all my hard work on the cupboard'.) Moving along the assertiveness continuum I also find myself saying from time to time, in a calm tone of voice, 'I worked hard on that dinner, and you took a second serving—it would be nice if you could at least comment that you liked it.' (Instead of, 'Two hours I spent shopping and cooking and scrubbing saucepans and I receive no appreciation whatsoever!') Tomek has definitely improved on this latter issue. I could probably improve on my frequency of thanking him for working so many hours to help provide for the family.

MAKE PEACE WITH HOUSEWORK

Not only is it possible to demonise a partner who does not do enough housework, it is also possible to demonise housework itself, labelling it annoying, crazy-making, a nuisance. A Zen approach of clear-seeing can be healing here. Clear-seeing, for Zen Buddhists, means seeing a task as nothing other than what it is. It is 'just sweeping', 'just vacuuming', 'just scrubbing a saucepan'. We make the task troublesome to our mind when we 'add' interpretations. Instead of 'just sweeping', we tell ourselves that sweeping is 'boring', 'unpaid', or 'something I should have delegated to that lazy schmuck on the couch'. We add so very much to the simple act of sweeping and the adding robs us of any sense of peace and calm.

I sometimes catch snatches of a light and comical radio segment in the afternoon and on one occasion they offered listeners the opportunity to ring in and confess, or 'come out', about a secret love of sweeping. Plenty of people rang and talked about how soothing, calming and even addictive they found the act of sweeping. It goes to show that any negative interpretations of the act of sweeping, or any household chore, are not inevitable, let alone 'the truth'. To a large extent, the experience of housework can be like a blank slate—we can make of it whatever we choose to. In past books I have quoted Buddhist friend Camilla who, by being mindful, has turned the repetitive rhythms of housework into meditative gestures: 'As a meditation, housework is very effective because it's simple. My accounting work takes so much mental effort so it's harder to bring mindfulness to it. With physical work, I find that I can really meditate doing that.' Rather than suppress negative thoughts about housework, we can practise mindfulness: notice the negative thoughts and instead of buying into them and believing them, treat them as clouds passing across a blue sky. Then we let them go.

It's also worth sparing a thought for our karma at this point. I described in the last chapter how karma is about the intention behind our actions. Our intentions plant seeds in our minds and the seeds ripen at various points in the future. This means our intention in any moment is important and affects our future.

My interpretation of the teaching of karma in relation to housework is that each moment that we let negative mind states reign—be it a dull, numb mind state, or an angry, or sad, or rushed mind state—we plant, and cultivate, seeds so that next time we do housework we are more likely to find ourselves in the same negative mind state. As Susan Maushart puts it in *Wifework*, 'All work and little play not only makes Mum a dull girl—it makes her a cranky one too.' The great challenge is, as Thich Nhat Hanh says, 'To water the seeds of joy'. If not joy, perhaps gratitude for your house and its contents, or peacefulness, love, kindness.

THINGS TO CONTEMPLATE . . .

- Do I spend enough time considering the difficulties and pressures my partner faces or do I mainly see my own?
- Do I feel, and express, gratitude for the contribution my partner makes around the house?
- Do I remember the causes and conditions contributing to an inequitable situation or do I demonise my partner and feel hostile?

- Which seeds do you water as you do the housework? The seeds of calmness? Peacefulness? Gratitude? Or the seeds of anger, numbness or stress?

THINGS TO DO

- Do address the issue of housework inequity but ensure you communicate skilfully, avoiding nagging, criticising and yelling.
- Keep in mind the gender roles you model for your children.
- While aiming to be assertive when appropriate, also consider accepting what is unlikely to change or what might drive you to insanity if you keep ruminating about it.
- When the time feels right, and when you do not feel too angry, remind your partner of any need you feel to hear appreciation of the housework you do.
- Express appreciation for the positive things your partner does for the household.
- Make peace with housework. See tasks clearly, for nothing other than what they are. Experiment with a meditative approach.

CHAPTER 7

communication

ONE MORNING I OPENED a tin of white paint and wrote on our kitchen tiles in huge letters, 'SARAH IS ALWAYS RIGHT'. I then sat back with my coffee to enjoy the shocked reaction of family members as they arrived for breakfast.

That was fun.

Our floor was being retiled that day but, in retrospect, I feel bemused: of all the things I could have written I chose that. It was definitely a good summary of my approach to marriage at that time. While there is nothing wrong with a little playful, light-hearted point-scoring, I know that with Tomek and I this can disintegrate into a whole way of life where every interaction is a competition to be right—sometimes fun and stimulating, at other times exasperating and alienating.

We assume that being right makes us the winner when, often enough, we only undermine the quality of relationship. We reinforce the 'me versus you' mentality, the delusion of 'self and other'. Opting for wins in the short term, we have only moved further away from the higher goal of loving connection. We win battles and lose wars. These days I try to be aware of when our conversation has become a battle to be right. If I can catch myself in time, this awareness is all I need in order to let go and aim higher. I have found, rather often, it doesn't hurt a bit.

AM I BEHAVING LIKE A GIRAFFE OR A JACKAL?

Last night at my Buddhist group, one of the members, Robin, a psychotherapist and marriage counsellor, gave a talk introducing us to animal characters from the widely practised field called Nonviolent Communication, sometimes referred to as Compassionate Communication. The giraffe, Robin explained, is considered the animal with the most heart. With its long neck it has access to a wider perspective, a bigger picture, so it focuses on the feelings and personal needs of the self and the other. The jackal, on the other hand, is an animal who barks and attacks unexpectedly. He fancies himself as a diagnoser of problems, the ultimate judge of good/bad, right/wrong, normal/abnormal. Where the jackal blames and thinks it has a monopoly on 'the truth', the giraffe is empathic, honest and non-blaming. Even when under attack the giraffe asks, 'What unmet needs are behind this attack?' The giraffe makes requests, where the jackal makes demands.

Compare these conversations, the first between two people speaking jackal:

Jackal 1: 'You never listen to me!'
Jackal 2: 'If you ever said anything interesting, maybe I would.'

Both jackals are left feeling an abyss of separation between them. In the second conversation, a giraffe responds calmly to the jackal:

Jackal: 'You never listen to me!'
Giraffe: 'I didn't mean to make you feel invisible. Tell me what
I can do to help you feel more heard.'

This time, rather than take offence and defend the self, the giraffe focuses on unmet needs, in this case the need to be acknowledged rather than feel invisible. The giraffe then expresses concern by being open and receptive to their partner's ideas. This almost seems like a Sunday school lesson: we all know the answer to the question 'Which one is the most effective communicator?' The founder of Nonviolent Communication, Marshall Rosenberg, describes this form of communication as something we already know how to do but that we forget because: 'We are educated to play the game called, "Who is right?" But in that game everybody loses. Jackal language cuts us off from life by blocking us from what is called "natural giving" where we experience the joy of giving to another.'[1]

Many of us choose to communicate like a couple of jackals even though, if asked, we would support more empathic forms of communication. If we can remember to focus on needs other than our need to be right, other than the need to defend the self, then communication will work to enhance our relationship. And mutual compassion will arise more easily.

PROVIDING SPACE

When tensions are high I do not so much listen to Tomek as assume, *I already know exactly what he's going to say, I've heard it a thousand times.* I then talk over the top of him, and he me. Unhappy couples tend to lament that they don't feel heard in the relationship, that they don't feel understood, or that their partner just doesn't listen. Thinking our partner does not see us clearly—our longings, our needs, our sensitivities—can be lonely. Before considering some of the deeper reasons that people can feel unheard, let's start with the most obvious cause: often we interrupt each other, cutting each other off mid-message. We do not make any space to even hear a complete sentence.

My meditation group received feedback that more confident and articulate group members dominated our discussions. In response, we began a practice of passing an object, currently a conch shell, around the group and whoever holds the shell has the floor, uninterrupted. Everybody has a chance to contribute and quieter members have a chance to express themselves if they choose. The only price is we all go home later, but nobody seems to mind. Couples therapists also use this approach, advising a couple to pass an object back and forth between them, to encourage each person to listen, without interrupting, to whoever is talking.

Such a strategy would feel a tad unnatural for Tomek and me, but we can still learn from the approach. Instead of passing an object back and forth, I consciously, and literally, bite my tongue. The sensation of biting is a reminder to be mindful and attentive and allow Tomek to finish his point. Tension dissolves because Tomek does not feel cut off halfway through his message.

It then helps even further if, before launching into my argument, I say something like, 'Okay, I can see your point that . . . so here's what I think . . .' In other words, if I can paraphrase what he has said back to him, then he feels especially 'heard' and tensions abate. During conflicts, what fuels our frustration is our sense that our partner does not hear our message: *I'm just not getting through to him, It goes in one ear and out the other, It's like talking to a brick wall.* To hear our message paraphrased back to us can remove considerable angst from a discussion.

Expressing our partner's point of view

For the last four years I have learnt more about communication in close relationships by doing a few hours a month as a volunteer on a phoneline. Run by an organisation called Family Drug Support, the line was set up in 1997 to support family members of people with drug and alcohol problems. In many cases, there is little callers can do to immediately solve their problems, which often involve substance dependence in a user who, for the time being, may have no desire to give up. One area—often the only area—callers can focus on is the quality of their communication with the drug user.

A drug- or alcohol-dependent family member causes anguish for those who love them, and it is easy and typical to resort to angry responses such as yelling and threatening. Yet locking horns with the user tends to only entrench the situation. A confrontational style forces them to defend their position and doing so only reminds them of all the positive aspects of their substance use.

As volunteers, we often find ourselves teaching the callers a different way to communicate that can seem counterintuitive at first. On so many calls I find myself saying—and have indeed been trained to say—something like what follows. Here is a hypothetical reply I might make to a husband who has just explained his concerns about his wife's increasing use of synthetic drugs:

Most people in your position will tell their wife that she is ruining her life, her health, her future, and taking terrible risks. When your wife hears that she might ignore or dismiss you because she thinks you are overreacting. Or she might argue with you and defend her substance use. If you say black, she'll say white, over and over again, and there is no progress.

Another option, and I realise this can go against the grain, is to let your wife know that you understand some of the benefits to her of drug-taking. You can say, for example, 'I can understand it helps you to forget your problems'. Or, 'I realise it causes chemical reactions in the brain that make you feel really, really good.' Or, 'Taking the drug probably helps you to feel like you belong to a group who all have something in common.' Or, 'I know you were feeling bored in your job and taking the drug and hanging out with those people probably feels really exciting in comparison.'

There are several benefits to expressing these positives. Firstly, your wife will feel more understood and that might help her open up to you. Secondly, because you are suddenly expressing arguments from her side it short circuits the repetitive arguments where you say black and she says white. This might just create the space for a more constructive conversation to begin.

Finally, the ideal outcome, which may or may not happen, is that your mentioning the benefits will induce her to start talking, or thinking, about the drawbacks rather than just reflexively defending her drug use. Of course, you can still talk about your worries, but your wife is more likely to listen if she thinks you understand her attraction to the drug too.

If we can convey to someone that we truly understand their viewpoint, even if we don't agree with it, they feel the relief of being understood and become more open to exploring the issue and considering alternative points of view. This approach is useful for more issues than only substance abuse. We could apply it to several of the most common disputes in relationships such as money, sex, housework and approaches to parenting.

SKILFUL SPEECH . . . WITHOUT GOING ON AND ON

The Buddha certainly thought communication was important because he made Skilful Speech a component of his Eightfold Path, even though it could easily have been folded into Skilful Action. The Buddha likened the tongue to 'an axe in our mouths' that can harm ourselves and others. He advised us to use speech that was: 'truthful, useful, spoken at the right time and motivated by compassion'. I particularly appreciate 'spoken at the right time'. For me this means not to bring something contentious up as soon as Tomek walks in the door from work, nor when either of us feel exhausted, nor when the children are around, nor when anyone is in a bad mood or feeling stressed. This doesn't leave much time to raise an issue but sometimes it is well worth waiting for a better time, if not dropping a gripe altogether.

Now, I have to admit, this chapter on communication is a little shorter than other chapters. So maybe I should show my cards at this point and admit I find communication a boring topic. Yes, the Buddha thought that skilful speech was important enough to include as a separate category in the Eightfold Path, but he didn't go on and on about how it was done. I, too, think our style of communication is incredibly important but don't most of us already 'get' what makes good communication? Most socially functioning people communicate amicably at work and with friends, minding our manners, avoiding conflict, not raising our voice. I suspect that poor communication within our partnerships is not so much a problem of knowhow but a matter of strong emotions gaining the upper hand. Emotions affect our body language and intonation and these two convey far more than the actual words we choose.

I sometimes wonder if the emphasis on 'communication', as evidenced by all the books and courses about it, is a little like our overvaluing of 'thinking'. Just as we tend to assume we can 'think' our way to the perfect, problem-free life, many of us assume we can 'talk' our way to the perfect, problem-free relationship. I suspect more relationship spats are resolved by the passage of time rather than by talking. In the worst cases, a poor partner endures a barrage of words that only makes them feel drained and desperate to escape. (Just ask Tomek.) There's a lot to be said for a 'concise' message. For some of us, this might mean planning our wording in advance.

I have looked at the literature on communication in partnerships and attended the odd workshop over the years and it is my view that all that advice on resolving issues through communication boils down to ten points that don't need chapters and chapters of elaboration. This is my summary:

- Stick to one point. Don't discuss all your problems at once. You don't have time.
- Be specific. Describe examples of *behaviour* rather than personal flaws.
- Speak about how things feel for you ('I feel upset when I find the kitchen in a mess so often'). No one can argue with how you feel.
- Avoid blaming ('You never clean up. You don't care about anyone but yourself').
- Ban the words 'always' and 'never'. Very inflammatory.
- Avoid sounding critical, contemptuous or exaggerated.
- Dwell more on the future than the past. How will things be from now on?
- Be open to how you, yourself, can improve things. Accept responsibility ('I'll try to . . .').
- With emotional issues, spend some time listening and providing empathy ('That sounds hard . . .') before launching into fixing mode.
- Call an adjournment if discussion becomes too heated.

THINGS TO CONTEMPLATE . . .

- Do I get carried away with the need to win an argument or be 'right' at the expense of the quality of my connection with my partner?
- Do I truly listen to my partner, allowing time and space for them to make their point, or do I interrupt—or use their speaking time to plan my next point?

- Are there any techniques I could use (biting my tongue, passing an object back and forth, explicit requests) to ensure we both listen to each other?

THINGS TO DO

- Especially during more tense conversations, try to identify the unmet needs of yourself and your partner.
- Ask yourself if now is the right time to address a tricky issue.
- Refer to the ten tips on the previous page.

CHAPTER 8

reducing stress
and anxiety

WHEN I WAS IN my twenties I kept a notepad in which to record inspiring quotations. Leafing through those pages, twenty years later, I note that a disproportionate number of the quotations came from a book called *The Heart of Buddhism* by Guy Claxton. This book provided my first glimpse into the Buddha's teachings and, re-reading them today, I recall my original excitement. Here is a sample of three quotations that introduced me to the novel idea that my external conditions did not need to limit my happiness:

> The more closely I hitch my contentment to my conditions, the more at risk I am when the unexpected or the unwanted happens—as it must.

> Buddha's deep realisations were just how much of our suffering is self-inflicted, and just how much elbow room we have to dissociate our serenity from our situation—not by perfecting our defences, but by seeing that defence is unnecessary.

> Suffering only hurts because you fear it, and complain about it. It pursues you because you flee from it . . . It is only your aversion that hurts, nothing else.[1]

I remember feeling so liberated by these words. Suddenly it was clear that I had so much more power over my capacity to enjoy my life than I had always believed. Instead of seeing myself as this entity that things happened to, I realised that the entity could choose her reactions. I finally saw that so much of my 'suffering' had indeed been self-inflicted because I often chose to believe my most dramatic and ridiculous thoughts. I realised that contentment could be cultivated within myself and that it need not be fully determined by events outside me or the behaviour of those around me. Of course, the power of my past conditioning would make it hard to fully benefit from these teachings: I would need to cultivate mindfulness of my thoughts so that I could realise when I had become caught up in my own reactivity.

It can also help us in family life if we continue to ask ourselves: how much of my frustration with my partner, and family, is self-inflicted? Are my reactions inevitable such that everybody would respond the same way in my situation? Could I choose different reactions? Does the mess, the chaos, the rush, actually hurt me, or is it my aversion to it that makes me feel so rattled?

What could I let go of in order to reduce my suffering?

A SPACIOUS MIND

Tomek is highly intelligent in a lop-sided, left-brained way and suffers the same problem as many of the highly intelligent: the feeling that he is surrounded by idiots. It's not easy for us idiots either. If his mood is irritable, Tomek can be impatient when he finds me slow to understand what he says or when I misinterpret him. If he expresses this impatience when my mindfulness is faint I can feel suddenly sad and anxious. While I might feel angry towards him I also blame myself: *Maybe I'm really stupid and vague . . . or not good enough . . . like generally. I really should have understood what he was saying. I wonder if other people would have understood him straight away. Yikes. Shit. What's wrong with me?*

This is an example of why it is worth cultivating a more spacious mind. We often associate meditation with calmness but another quality it cultivates that can play a part in reducing our stress levels is spaciousness of mind. My favourite metaphor illustrating the effect of spaciousness is this one: if we add a teaspoon of poison to a cup of water then the water becomes contaminated, but if we add a teaspoon of poison to a lagoon, it has little effect. Similarly, if our partner makes a careless comment when our mind is spacious, we feel little effect. If our mind is contracted and small, then any insensitive remark feels like a declaration of war.

We can cultivate spaciousness of mind during a meditation sit, or as mindfulness brought into our daily life. Remember that mindfulness is non-judgemental, conscious awareness of whatever is happening. Mindfulness is translated from the Pali word '*sati*', which we could literally translate as 'memory'. The thing the Buddha wanted us to remember was the present. When we become lost in our thoughts, we have forgotten the present. So we *remember* 'now' rather than follow the distractions of thoughts about the past and future. And if we do find ourselves thinking about the past or the future, then we can pay attention to those thoughts, observe where they go, as opposed to being lost in them. Opportunities to practise mindfulness include when we wait at traffic lights, or in queues, or for our computer to start. We can be mindful as we chop vegetables, hang out washing, walk down a street.

In Buddhism there are six senses through which we perceive life: sight, smell, touch, taste, hearing and the mind. For the latter, we can practise mindfulness of our thoughts about our relationship. Long-term relationships can sometimes feel dull or stuck in a rut but with mindfulness we try to see our habitual thoughts and reactions clearly, but non-judgementally, and this makes us more open. As our minds become more spacious we might open ourselves to something greater: a more expansive view of ourselves, our partner, or our relationship. We might see the potential, the myriad possibilities before us, only visible when we let go of grudges, resentments, attachments, when we open to love, in all its vastness.

If my mind was spacious I would perceive Tomek's momentary impatience as *his* problem, which it is. I might even laugh at the situation, or laugh at myself. Refusing to take ourselves too seriously is very, very mentally healthy. With a spacious mind, we are more likely to see that we can choose our reactions. With a contracted mind we feel our reaction is the only one available, that it is inevitable. With a spacious mind I can admit that I too can be impatient with Tomek. Or that his impatience takes place over a few seconds and need not preoccupy me for hours. Or that I should toughen up a bit and stop playing the wounded child (but still maintain self-compassion!).

When we consider just how many potential irritants and offences exist in family life, there is no end to it. We cannot change all these irritating details so that circumstances remain in a state to our liking, or under control. We need to develop our awareness of how much of our suffering is self-inflicted and how much we could let go of. This is especially the case if we are perfectionists, insisting on a continually tidy house, or well-behaved occupants. While we can make every effort to adjust conditions to our liking, becoming attached to the results of our efforts does not lead to contentment. Some Buddhists I know repeat a mantra, 'patience with conditions'.

FINDING CALM THROUGH MEDITATION

One thing is sure. We can read all the books, immerse ourselves in Buddhist teachings, even make a commitment to prioritise our relationship, but if our stress levels are too high, our fuse will remain short. We snap at our partner because we feel pressured, anxious or overwhelmed. Or we withdraw from human contact for extended periods. Few of us can afford to take our stress out on people at work, on friends, or strangers, so family becomes the dumping ground. Then, of course, we don't want to damage our children too much, so that leaves our partner to bear the brunt of our burdens.

In times of high stress, we need to acknowledge to ourselves and our family members that our reactions to daily irritations are more about our state of stress than the irritations themselves. Otherwise we become blamers—and blaming mode tends to fuel stress and make everyone feel worse. One alternative is to admit to our partner, or other family members, 'I'm feeling stressed at the moment,' and then they know they need not take our mood, and its effects on our behaviour, too personally.

We also need to ensure we have some tools to calm ourselves, to lengthen those fuses, especially if we are powerless, for the time being, to reduce our load. The Buddha taught mindfulness not only as a path to calmness but to purification and an end to *dukkha*. The teaching included mindfulness of:

- the body
- feelings (pleasant, unpleasant or neutral)
- mental states (such as angry, scattered, concentrated, or clear)
- the teachings (the Four Noble Truths, the Eightfold Path, the three poisons of greed, hatred and delusion, and many more).

As part of mindfulness of the body the Buddha taught us the simple technique known as mindfulness of the breath. In his words:

Breathing in long, he knows 'I breathe in long,' breathing out long, he knows 'I breathe out long.' Breathing in short, he knows 'I breathe in short,' breathing out short, he knows 'I breathe out short.' He trains thus: 'I shall breathe in experiencing the whole body'; he trains thus: 'I shall breathe out experiencing the whole body'. He trains thus: 'I shall breathe in calming the bodily formation'; he trains thus: 'I shall breathe out calming the bodily formation.'

While the Buddha suggests mindfulness of the breath be done in the cross-legged meditation posture, at the root of a tree or in an empty hut, it is a practice we can bring to whatever posture, and whatever place we find ourselves in.

My experience of meditation as it is practised in the Theravadin, or 'Insight', tradition is that mindfulness of the breath is an excellent starting point for practice, especially for developing serenity. Yet most of the meditators I have known eventually branch out into other techniques. They might use the technique of non-judgementally labelling their experiences in meditation with words such as, 'thinking', 'feeling', 'anger' or 'tired'. They may practise the technique called 'choiceless awareness', where they are aware of whatever experiences arise in the moment, whether it be a thought, an itch, a mood, a sound, or a story playing in their mind.

Many teachers also encourage us to not be attached to our technique, or our teacher, and to remain watchful of the effects of our technique for they all have potential downfalls. The Buddha taught that every single phenomenon, even a meditation technique, is marked by *dukkha*, by unsatisfactoriness. For example, people who cling to the technique of mindfulness of the breath might find they block or exclude emotional experiences that need their attention. People who practise lovingkindness meditation might find themselves imposing a loving feeling on themselves and denying how they truly feel. People who practise choiceless awareness might find themselves lost, or dull, and could benefit from a more focused approach such as returning to mindfulness of the breath or body.

Meditation techniques all tend to be simple so it is almost comical the number of ways we can complicate them, leading many to claim, 'I can't meditate!' Here are some common ways we sabotage a meditation session:

- **We add expectations.** *Shouldn't I be feeling blissed out? Or calm? Or happy? I want to have deep insights!* We need to let go of any expectations and sit with *what is*, open to whatever mind state arises. Meditation will be different for everyone and different every time we sit.

- **We add fantasies about how meditation will change us in a prescribed way.** *I meditate to become more kind, less angry, more together.* This is attachment: attachment to a new, improved self. We may even think to ourselves, *Perhaps others will notice, appreciate and admire my new, improved self.* Some treat meditation as a way to remove what they hate about themselves rather than a practice of self-acceptance. Meditation is not a self-improvement program. We are already whole. All we need is already inside us.

- **We add goals.** *I must have a spiritual experience. I must eliminate anger. I will become joyous.* Attachment is the cause of our suffering. We are not in pursuit of something when we meditate. Rather, we cultivate letting go, freedom from desire. Sometimes when I sit, I set an intention, *Being nobody, going nowhere, wanting nothing.*

- **We impose pleasant moods.** *I'm doing this to feel better! I want to be calm.* We believe we should feel a certain way, and we try to impose reassuring states such as joy, love or calmness. Some teachers would call this spiritual bypassing, where, rather than sit with what arises in the moment and what therefore deserves our non-judgemental attention, we pretend that everything is lovely and spiritual. We could do this for years and never gain any self-awareness or insight. Of course, there is no need to suppress a pleasant feeling if it arises, and many believe it is worth actively generating pleasant mind states. Still, many a teacher would advise us to be there for the less pleasant experiences as well for they have much to teach us.

- **We block experiences as 'not meditation'.** *I found myself feeling angry, so I started doing lovingkindness meditation. I felt sad so I forced myself to focus on my breath and block out that feeling.* In meditation we need exclude nothing. If something 'not nice' arises, then it is grist for the mill. If relationship problems arise, rage, grief, sexual fantasies, we mindfully sit with whatever comes up. We provide the space and proceed to *be with* our experience. Yes, we might become lost in our experiences but we can still learn from that too. Many of us fear we might lose control if we let strong emotions run their course. Yet when we bring awareness to them, and watch them unfurl, we learn they are fleeting and insubstantial and not 'who we are'.

- **We feel a sense of failure.** *I couldn't stop my thoughts! I'm utterly incapable of concentrating!* Thoughts are no indication that you are 'doing it wrong' or that you are not cut out for meditation. Thinking is what the mind does. When thoughts arise, we treat them as clouds passing across a blue sky without judging them, or clinging to them, and we return to the breath. Or if we are using a more insight-oriented technique, we do not return to the breath but continue to watch the thoughts, non-judgementally, adding nothing.

·

Admittedly, it can be confusing: 'I want to cultivate generosity, calmness, love but I'm not supposed to have any goals.' One Buddhist teacher, Victor von der Heyde, prefers the term 'soft goal' or 'intention'. He explains a gentler approach: 'Meditation might be like walking through a park towards a destination. In any moment, you are focused on walking in the park and you feel no particular attachment to the destination. Sure, it would be nice to arrive at the destination on the other side of the park, but it won't be a big deal if you don't.'

Victor had the opportunity to meditate in Nepal in a group of practitioners from both East and West. The teacher gave meditation instructions, and told the Nepalis and Tibetans to closely stick to and follow the instructions. Then he told the Westerners to follow the instructions about 70 per cent. The teacher said that Westerners tend to sabotage their meditation by trying too hard, by focusing too much on a goal, by succumbing to their all-consuming need to 'get it right'. Victor encourages meditators to remember to keep their approach light, and if possible to include an element of playfulness. He also recommends cultivating a degree of warmth, adding that some teachers use the word, 'kindfulness'. We need to be kind to ourselves as we meditate, aware of when we are too judgemental, or critical, so that we can let go and ease up on ourselves.

In meditation we treat ourselves with gentleness, patience and love. We might even find compassion for our inner critic who tells us we are such a lousy meditator. We practise noticing her comments and her tone, non-judgementally, and we eventually realise she's not as smart as she thinks she is.

AND IF OUR PARTNER IS NOT OPEN TO MEDITATION AS A WAY TO CALM DOWN . . .

I once met a kindly old man, long retired, who told me his wife would not let him into the house after work unless he had stopped off at the pub for a quick drink first. 'She told me she could not put up with me if I came straight home from work,' he laughed. 'She said I had to unwind before I could be any use to her and the children.' While stopping off at the pub is not exactly a Buddhist solution for partners arriving home from work frazzled, there is still wisdom in this scenario. The wisdom lies in creating a transition period between work and home.

The transition period may consist of five minutes resting in the car, or the front porch, taking some deep breaths, or consciously relaxing the body, before walking into the house. Even just one minute helps us let go of the day at work. A hot bath after work, or a walk around the block may provide the transition. We may lose a small amount of family time with our partner, but if such an investment improves the quality of that time by allowing for some stress release then it may be worth it. This mother decided to try this approach:

My husband tended to arrive home from work every day with a frown on his face and I would feel my own tension rise when he walked into the house. While I had the option of telling him that I hate this, it occurred to me that I could frame my complaint as an act of generosity so I said: 'You seem to be tense from work when you arrive home. Why don't you treat yourself to five minutes sitting in the car with your eyes closed so that you get a little break.'

Alternatively, exercise might diffuse the stresses of the day.

PHYSICAL EXERCISE AND THE RELATIONSHIP

For some of us, not all, regular physical exercise is highly relevant to our relationship. Tomek and I, for example, occupy the two extremes of the spectrum. I am highly dependent on regular exercise in order to feel comfortable in my body. Without it, I feel restless, frustrated and desperate for a stretch. Without it, I cannot count on a good night of sleep and I am more likely to turn to sugary snacks for comfort—which make me feel worse—so beginning a downward spiral into snappiness with those around me. With exercise so important to my mood, it plays a significant role in transforming my mind into that spacious lagoon in which the drops of poison, the small irritations of daily life and relationships, have less impact.

My dependence on exercise, sadly, does not arise out of any talent for sport. Tomek, on the other hand, has some great achievements in the sporting arena (even refereeing European handball at the Sydney Olympics!). Yet he claims that exercise makes no difference to his mood, or how his body feels and at this stage of his life he does not miss it one iota. He is now one of those people of whom they say, 'If the urge to exercise ever comes over him, he sits down and waits for it to pass.' He seems to have enough exercise credits from his past to see him through middle age without paying too high a price for his sedentary lifestyle.

So the task is to recognise where we are on this spectrum of 'need for exercise' and to find ways to ensure we fulfil our needs. Failing this, as the exercise-dependent often will, we bring awareness to the effect on our body, take responsibility for it and refrain from taking out our physical discomfort on those around us. Our body and general mood are also affected to varying degrees by diet, how much rest we need and even by how much meaningful human interaction, or solitude, we need. The Buddha advised a middle path between the extremes of self-denial and over-indulgence: 'To keep our body in good health is a duty otherwise we shall not be able to keep the mind strong and clear.'

It is also worth considering the extent to which the form of exercise we choose is helpful to our spiritual practice. I have enjoyed bushwalking, and running, for the way they allow mindfulness of nature and surroundings. However, Pilates and yoga are excellent for bringing awareness back to the body. Body-awareness, and the sense of presence that goes with it, helps to make us more grounded and emotionally stable throughout the day.

At the yoga class I attend, the instructor regularly reminds us as we stretch to let go of thoughts about our 'to do' list, or about our worries, and to concentrate on our breath, find our inner stillness and quieten the mind. We 'breathe into any place of tightness, releasing any tension'. For the rest of the day, I feel lighter, more ready to laugh, more patient with family members, my mind more like the spacious lagoon.

THINGS TO CONTEMPLATE . . .

- How dependent am I on my external conditions to feel content? What scope is there to turn inward and find peace, even joyfulness, within?
- Do I see myself as a victim of circumstances? Can I see the potential to choose more of my reactions instead of assuming they are inevitable?

THINGS TO DO

- Start asking yourself, 'How much of my experience of suffering is self-inflicted?'
- Use meditation, or mindfulness in our daily lives, to cultivate a spacious mind that is not offended by every hint of criticism.
- Admit to your partner if you feel exhausted or stressed so that they feel no need to take your mood personally.

- Practise non-attachment to your meditation technique and your teacher. Nothing is perfect. Everything changes.
- Be aware of the common pitfalls—especially for Westerners—of meditation: expectations, goals, imposing moods, blocking experiences that need our attention, feeling like a failure, trying too hard.
- Encourage a frazzled partner to take a few minutes alone before joining the family.
- Tune in to the needs of your body and recognise the duty to attend to exercise, nutrition and rest. Consider also whether you have achieved the right balance between the need to associate with others and to bask in solitude. Ignoring our health, be it physical or emotional, threatens our capacity to be present and compassionate.
- Consider forms of exercise that complement a spiritual practice: walk with mindfulness of the surroundings, stretch with body awareness, run with joy (if you can).

CHAPTER 9

who is our partner?

Ours is a generation highly focused on the art of parenting. Many of us give considerable mental space to assessing our adequacy as a parent and feel crushing guilt when we fail to meet our expectations. The worst insult we can imagine is to be labelled a 'bad parent' as it strikes at the heart of our identity. Focusing on extreme cases, media commentators decry 'hovering parents' and 'helicopter parents' who are over-involved in their children's lives, denying them the autonomy they need to grow.

Extremes aside, I personally feel grateful to be part of a generation capable of reflecting on their parenting, one that cares about their children's emotional adjustment and mental health so much more than the generations of the past did. Even still, the modern preoccupation with parenting can come at the expense of the attention we give to our partner. I have certainly been guilty of this myself. My preoccupation with my role as a mother has meant that Tomek's needs, at times, have barely appeared on my radar.

Even if we have given our relationship sufficient priority, a couple can still be starved of quality time together. The details of running a household and the logistics of who will drive which child where dominate our conversations. A quick debrief of the events of our day can be the greatest conversational height we reach. When our relationship has been reduced to rushed exchanges it is easy to take each other for granted, to become careless about how we communicate, to perceive our partner as a mere mechanism in the running of the household.

We might see our partner only in terms of how well they meet our needs, practical and emotional. We stop seeing our partner for who they are, in this moment, and relate to an outdated image we created long ago. Like ourselves though, our partner is constantly, if subtly, changing and so warrants our attention afresh with each new day. We need to remember to *be* with our partner, ensuring we make time to pause occasionally and let go of doing, negotiating, judging, so that we can just 'see' who our partner is in this very moment. This fresh way of looking is a mark of respect for our partner. Not many people realise the word respect comes from the Latin root *'spec'*, which means to see; add the prefix re- and the word respect translates as 'to see again'.

PERCEIVING OUR PARTNER MORE CLEARLY

Some of us see our partners as a mass of flaws. At the worst of times, we see our partner as a drain on our energy or as best avoided. We may perceive them in terms of an exchange relationship: as someone who gives *this* much and takes *that* much. Whichever way we perceive our partner, it is likely to be a misperception, or at least an incomplete perception of who they truly are.

Allow me to quote again from that first book I ever read on Buddhism, *The Heart of Buddhism* by Guy Claxton (who was quoting Herman Hesse): 'The man who I look at with dread or hope, with greed, designs or demands, is not a man but a cloudy mirror of my own desire.'[1] Over the years, I would occasionally catch myself relating to others with nothing but concern for my own needs—for acceptance, approval, affection or company—and no thought for theirs. The words 'cloudy mirror of my own desire' would wake me up, reminding me that the person in question was an individual quite apart from what I wanted from them.

Bizarrely, studies have found that those married for many years perceive their partner with less accuracy than newlyweds do.[2] Newlyweds scored higher results than the long-married when it came to inferring what their partner was thinking and feeling. The researchers presumed this to be due to a decline over time in our motivation to understand our partner and, therefore, in the amount of attention we pay them. As a relationship progresses we assume we know all there is to know. We can turn our partner into a fixed object, especially if we spend large amounts of time ruminating on their flaws. With an inflexible, rigid view, we fail to notice new information.

With Buddhist practice we aim to be open, present and curious about our partner. We might aim to perceive our partner as a 'mystery', rather than as a crystallised set of characteristics, because we tend to respond to mysteries with an attitude of curiosity: we listen and engage deeply. We can try regarding our partner as a riddle, as a Zen koan. A koan is a meditation tool, a problem or riddle that has no solution. The most well-known example is, 'What is the sound of one hand clapping?' The only answer to a koan is to give up on thinking as a way to find a solution, and, in the case of our partner, relate to the other in the present moment with a beginner's mind. Someone who clearly understands this way of relating is Colombian novelist Gabriel García Márquez, who said of his wife of fifty years that he knows her 'a little less with each passing year, as she becomes more and more the mystery she always was'.

Remembering to look at our partner with this new, non-judgemental, open approach is difficult. Just as it is difficult to remember to practise mindfulness, it is also difficult to remember to look on our partner with a beginner's mind. It is up to each of us to challenge ourselves: what can I do to help myself remember this way of looking more often?

One thing that can help us perceive our partner more accurately is to clear our view of them of some of our attachments, or cravings. In his brilliant book, *Insight Dialogue: The interpersonal path to freedom*, Buddhist teacher Gregory Kramer writes about attachment, the cause of suffering, or as he translates it, 'hunger':

When we are hungry, we see other people primarily as potential food, not as who they are in and of themselves. Also, when we are experiencing relational pleasure, we may be afraid of losing it, and so we act selfishly to protect what is 'ours'. When we can't get the pleasure we want, we get hurt and then angry . . . This hunger for pleasure imbues our lives with a feeling of lack, dissatisfaction, and incompletion. The hunger, by its very nature, will never be lastingly fulfilled, only temporarily satisfied.[3]

With the fading of these hungers, which comes from letting go, Kramer writes, 'social life becomes compassionate encounter rather than an effort to gain pleasurable stimulation, uphold an image or dodge the gaze of others'.

The Buddha spoke of three types of craving: the craving for sensual pleasure, the craving for being and for non-being. The craving for being is understood as the craving to exist, the survival instinct, while the craving for non-being is the craving for escape from life, or oblivion. Kramer sees interpersonal equivalents for the three cravings:

- The craving for sensual pleasure equates to a hunger for stimulation from others, or an expectation that they will remove unpleasant feelings such as loneliness or lack of fulfilment.
- The craving for being equates to a hunger 'to be seen' by others, or to have our existence confirmed.
- The craving for non-being is a hunger to 'not be seen' by others, such as when we avoid intimacy or withdraw into ourselves.

If we can become more aware of the cravings that dominate our partnership, how they play out and how they make us suffer, we gradually let go and make way for compassionate encounter.

MAKING SPACE FOR OUR PARTNER'S PERCEPTIONS

We would never admit it to anyone but most of us believe we are the centre of the universe. The world revolves around me; my perceptions and world view are correct. We never quite articulate what we secretly think: *If your world view is different to mine, if you perceive things differently and even think the world revolves around you, then you are just ignorant.* This is especially our attitude when we quietly believe we are just a little more intelligent, informed, expert, or experienced than our partner. Occasionally, perhaps years down the track, we can suddenly find ourselves surprised to discover our partner had been right about something all along.

It is worth looking at the increased potential for learning and insight that might come from considering how our partner perceives the world, from opening to their point of view. In Buddhist terms, such a process is called 'letting go of attachment to our own views'. Maybe our partner can see something that we cannot. If we are willing to cultivate some humility, and tune into our partner's perceptions, our world might well become a bigger, more interesting, more nuanced place. Zen Buddhism, in particular, emphasises the value of assuming an attitude of 'not knowing', of being prepared to say 'I don't know' more often. In a popular Zen parable, a master pours some tea into a new pupil's cup. 'That's enough, thank you,' says the pupil, but the teacher keeps pouring until the cup is overflowing with tea. 'Stop, stop,' yells the student in alarm. The master then says, 'How can I teach you anything new if your cup is already full?'

Tomek and I tend to hold different views on many issues, intellectual and personal, but this has often been a positive for our relationship. On an intellectual level, we both enjoy thrashing out our differences and we have both learnt many interesting points of view from each other. My views are more left wing than his, which is understandable since he left a country run by left-wing extremists. I believe he has helped me to be more pragmatic in my approach to political issues and I have helped him to be more compassionate.

On a personal level too, we can learn from our partner. Most of us, for example, will hear some criticism from our partner over the years. Our reflexive reaction is to defend ourselves, especially if our partner was insensitive about the way they chose to criticise us—if they relied, say, on nagging, yelling, snide comments or ridicule. Yet often there can be a sliver, if not a substantial slice, of truth in their criticism. Many a relationship progresses in great bounds after one partner is prepared to acknowledge the truth of some constructive criticism. Take this example from a man I met at a Buddhist event:

My wife used to always accuse me, on the way home from any social gathering, of flirting. She always complained, for example, that I would give all my attention to the most attractive female in the group and ignore everybody else. For years I saw these episodes as 'her jealousy problem'. Eventually, we attended a school function where I witnessed a man flirting with her and she appeared to be flirting back. I had this visceral reaction that shocked me but it finally dawned on me what my wife had been feeling all these years. I finally started trying to be more sensitive to her feelings at social gatherings.

It seems being open to your partner's perceptions has particularly encouraging results when men do it. Relationship 'guru', researcher John Gottman, found that one of the best predictors of a stable, happy marriage was a man's willingness to be influenced by his wife. The University of Washington Journal reported the results of Gottman's study:

'We found that only those newlywed men who are accepting of influence from their wives are winding up in happy, stable marriages,' said Gottman. 'Getting husbands to share power with their wives, by accepting some of the demands she makes, is critical in helping to resolve conflict.' Gottman said in the study that the wife usually brings marital issues up for discussion and she usually also presents an analysis of the problem and suggested solutions. Men who are able to accept their spouse's ideas are more likely to maintain a successful relationship.[4]

This finding is highly gratifying to women but the study also emphasised the need for women to 'soften the initial approach' when initiating a discussion, given the evidence that 'gentleness, compassion, and physiological soothing of partners are key ingredients that enable marriages to succeed'.

Any interaction with our partner can be a learning experience if we allow our partner to hold up a mirror for us. Living with a partner allows us to see how reactive we may be, how loving we are, how judgemental, how demanding. We can only learn from these interactions, however, if we are prepared to pause occasionally and reflect on them, if we are prepared to wake up from automatic patterns of relating, if we are prepared to be more mindful in our interactions. One mother decided to tune in more to her daily interactions with her husband only to notice a coldness there:

When I first met my husband, we always called each other honey or darling or sweetheart. After going through those early years of parenting, which for us were marked by distancing and resentment, we reverted back to using our first names. For us, I knew that our life together would start to feel more loving if we could reintroduce those more loving appellations. Little things like that can be powerful. I also tried to reintroduce into our busy lives small gestures like a brief caress of his arm or a quick rub of his back as we passed each other in the kitchen. Soon enough, he was reciprocating and our relationship feels more loving even though we are still short of extended periods of time together.

It is possible to be more loving even during the most routine interactions, and such small but affectionate gestures might just be exactly what our partner painfully yearns for.

SEEING BUDDHA NATURE

In his book *The Wise Heart*, Buddhist teacher Jack Kornfield reminds us that we have forgotten our essential nature, our original goodness and that of others too. We all function behind protective layers that block our Buddha Nature: 'Our belief in a limited and impoverished identity is such a strong habit that without it we are afraid we wouldn't know how to be . . . And yet some part of us knows that the frightened and damaged self is not who we are. Each of us needs to find our way to be whole and free.'[5]

Just as we limit our own sense of identity by seeing ourselves in habitual ways, we also limit our perception of others, not least our partner. Hence, Jack Kornfield urges us to 'see the inner nobility and beauty of all human beings'. He offers some tips for honouring the dignity of the other. We can imagine the other when they were a small child, precious and vulnerable. We can imagine the other as elderly, frail, or approaching death (remember that a Buddhist practice includes regular recognition of the certainty of death). Or we can look at the other's life right now and acknowledge the difficulties, the burdens.

On a Buddhist course I attended, the teacher set us an exercise to practise seeing the inner nobility of the people we interact with in our daily lives. Twenty or so of us were to walk slowly and mindfully around the room. When the gong sounded we turned to the nearest person and looked deeply into their eyes, recognising their uniqueness, their preciousness, their Buddha Nature. When we heard the gong again we continued our mindful walking until the next gong when we stared into the eyes of a different partner. The exercise continued and by the end we had all looked deeply into the eyes of eight or so people.

In the debrief, group members reported many positive feelings and had clearly developed an appreciation of the potential for 'sacred perception', which they intended to apply to their relationships in daily life.

Me, I felt traumatised.

I decided to tell Geoff about my experience at our next meeting. 'I just found the experience of staring silently into someone's eyes excruciating. I felt so self-conscious and awkward I wanted to disappear. But in the group debrief, everybody seemed to have enjoyed a completely positive experience.'

Part of me expected Geoff to perform a full-blown Freudian psychoanalysis complete with questions about my relationship with my mother. Yet Geoff generally prefers to soothe the voice of the drama queen and bring problems back into their proper perspective.

'I've got a feeling you weren't the only one in the room who felt a bit uncomfortable. There is a tendency in spiritual groups for everyone to enthuse about what they are experiencing but this can sometimes end up silencing other important voices that need to be heard as well.'

'So it's not just me?' I checked.

'My teacher, Joko, used to start every meeting with a meditation where we sat opposite each other staring into each other's eyes. And

I do remember finding that confronting. I don't think my reaction was as strong as yours, but at first it did feel unpleasant.'

'Yes, for me it felt almost unendurable,' I said.

'But I have to say that I became used to it and it helped me overcome a lot of shyness and self-consciousness.'

So Geoff was not going to appease my inner drama queen by diagnosing me with 'high levels of self-loathing', or 'insecure attachment issues'. I had to concede that the reasons for my painful self-consciousness probably came from having pimples and braces in my formative years.

'How have other people in your group found those types of exercises?' I asked, hoping for more evidence that I was not the only one who struggled with eye-gazing activities.

'I remember one woman suggested that staring into another's eyes is something you do only in the context of intimacy or aggression and because of these associations it feels like an intense thing to do.'

'So you could even say,' I suggested, 'that we have evolved, through human history, to find prolonged eye contact in silence to be an intense, and potentially unsettling experience.'

'Yes, you could. Of course Joko, my teacher, would have said that if that is your reaction, then work with that. Observe and learn from that rather than trying to impose a state that feels more correct. It is not wrong, or unspiritual, to have your reaction.'

When I returned to my course the next week, the teacher asked if we had practised seeing the inner nobility of others during our daily interactions. Many in the group had felt valuable shifts in their perspective on the people they lived with. Others in the group had forgotten, or had only remembered too late after an interaction was over. A few of us, curiously, found it easier to practise seeing the inner nobility in strangers and acquaintances than with those close to us. Our interactions with those close to us are far more stuck in automatic, habitual patterns.

Again, the challenge is remembering to do it. It's probably easier for Indians. Their word for both 'hello' and 'goodbye' is *namaste*, often accompanied by a small bow. A literal translation of the salutation is, 'I bow to the divine in you'.

I have been trying to see the Buddha Nature in Tomek, practising an inner bow, and can vouch that it pulls me out of automatic, unconsidered ways of perceiving him. Although it is unlikely we will ever engage in any eye-gazing activities together, I still have the option of quietly adopting such practices unilaterally for the benefit of us both.

POSITIVE ILLUSIONS?

A finding I kept coming across in psychology literature was that the happiest relationships were those marked by 'positive illusions', where at least one of the partners saw the other through rose-coloured glasses, idealising their qualities, downplaying their faults, excusing their mistakes, even assuming their relationship was superior to others.[6] I mulled over this finding a lot. These were couples who when asked 'Would you rather be happy or right?' chose happy. I thought through all the couples I had known and felt I had not met many who fitted this description over the longer term.

Moreover, this finding seemed contrary to the Buddha's teachings where the path out of suffering is about seeing clearly and accurately, by shedding our illusions. I ran this contradiction by Geoff who was sceptical about the finding although he did suggest a Buddhist perspective that could make sense of it:

I used to be quite critical of other people, which had a lot to do with being critical of myself. These days, especially as a therapist and as a Zen teacher, I do need to be capable of seeing the areas where people have blind spots or where they're stuck. Rather than being critical, though, I tend to see these aspects of people alongside their Buddha Nature. Practice isn't supposed to blind you to others' shortcomings . . . but the most realistic stance is to be able to see both: the blind spots and the Buddha Nature.

Perhaps if we are prepared to see the inner nobility of our partner, their Buddha Nature, alongside their flaws, then we too can have the so-called 'happier relationships'.

Granted, some may prefer to avoid intellectualising and simply adopt the late Nelson Mandela's view: 'It never hurts to think too highly of a person; often they become ennobled and act better because of it.'⁵

THINGS TO CONTEMPLATE . . .

- Does my commitment to being a good parent ever render my partner's needs invisible?
- Do I see my partner as a mere mechanism in the running of the household? As someone obliged to meet my needs rather than as a person in their own right?
- Does my perception of my partner need an update?
- Could I somehow make our daily interactions more loving and affectionate? In little ways?

THINGS TO DO

- Assume you do not fully know and understand your partner. See them as a mystery worthy of your curiosity.
- Be aware of attachments you may bring to your relationship such as to sensual pleasure, the desire to be seen or to hide. Try to gradually let go of these attachments in order to experience what Gregory Kramer calls 'compassionate encounter'.
- Increase your opportunities to grow and learn by opening to the way your partner perceives the world.
- Without beating yourself up, consider whether there might be some truth in your partner's complaints about you. (Remember self-compassion as you do this.)
- See the Buddha Nature, the inner nobility, of your partner when you look into their eyes. Try to perceive your partner's flaws or blind spots alongside this Buddha Nature.

CHAPTER 10

sex

WELCOME TO THE CHAPTER on sex. I suspect the occasional reader (you know who you are) has skipped previous chapters to be here. I'm guessing that one or two readers even bought *Buddhism for Couples* in the hope of learning some eastern secrets, as a possible gateway to, say, 'tantric sex'. If this is the case, I'm sorry to disappoint you. The Western concept of 'tantric sex' is a soup, or sludge, of concepts drawn from many different fields including, to a small extent, Tibetan Buddhism. Without doubt, tantric sex might help couples enhance their sex lives but Buddhism is not one of the major sources of it. Sex has a tiny role in the tantric Buddhism practised in Tibet but this is more about controlling sexual energy than letting it run riot. The goal is to channel sexual energy into becoming enlightened. Besides, these teachings are secret, only bestowed by celibate monks and only available to those well-ensconced in that Tibetan tradition. They involve loads of ritual and ceremony and even deities. I decided not to get involved.

Moreover, whatever Tibetan tantra can offer seems a long way from the kind of sexual issues modern Westerners grapple with, such as mismatched libidos, temptation from outside the relationship, lack of enjoyment, lack of time, or inability to relax. For those of us—most of us?—who struggle with sexual challenges we doubt there could be any simple, pat solutions to what can feel like unresolvable problems. My approach in this chapter has been to throw out a few different ideas and theories that, to my mind, chime with Buddhist teachings.

Do take the ideas in this chapter with a substantial grain of salt: none of them are necessarily 'right' or 'best' for you. They are only ideas, not great truths. Come to think of it, that advice applies to this whole book and, for that matter, the whole of Buddhism. After all, the Buddha himself said:

I am not teaching you to have you as my pupil. I am not interested to make you my pupil. I am not interested in breaking you from your old teacher. I am not interested even to change your goal, because everyone wants to come out of suffering. Try something that I have discovered, and then judge it for yourself. If it is good for you, accept it. Otherwise, don't accept it.

It is hard to write a chapter on sex for all possible readers. For many, sex is highly problematic and could well tie in with past trauma, be it child abuse, rape or memories of bad relationships. Other readers may feel completely 'over it', long past feeling interested in matters sexual, and if that is no problem for a partner, then feel free to skip the chapter. A lucky few might wonder why I have made such a simple, joyful act sound so complicated and fraught.

Complexity acknowledged, here goes.

COPING WITH DIFFERENT LIBIDOS

In 2009, sex therapist Bettina Arndt caused a stir with the release of her book *The Sex Diaries: Why women go off sex and other bedroom battles.*[1] Focusing on the problem of mismatched libidos, the book received plenty of publicity with excerpts published in major newspapers. Arndt drew from her experience as a sex therapist but also on the 'sex diaries' of 98 couples she had recruited. Controversially, Arndt suggested that women might consider having sex with their husband even when they were not in the mood. Her advice was not for women to suffer through unwanted sex. Rather, she proposed that desire and pleasure often kick in when women 'just do it'. She argues that as long as women can 'get their heads in the right place to anticipate pleasure', they may as well 'just do it'.

Heated conversations broke out in some of the circles I moved in. This one was in a living room at a baby shower I attended:

'Who does Bettina Arndt think she is? After all the hard work feminists have done to give women basic rights over their own bodies,' said one woman.

'I think she's just courting controversy to get attention and sell books,' said another.

'There's nothing worse than having sex against your will,' the first woman continued. 'No woman should have to endure that. Her advice is just so backward and anti-woman, I can't believe it is getting airplay in this day and age.'

A couple of weeks later at the school band camp, I found myself in a huddle of mothers who had come along as volunteer helpers. As I remember, the conversation went something like this:

'Sex with my husband is the great joy of my life. I just wish there was more time for it,' announced one mother who generally exudes confidence and *joie de vivre*. 'I think Bettina Arndt is right. Denying your husband sex is not fair. What man would marry you if he knew in advance that it would become a sexless marriage?'

'I agree, most men need sex,' chimed in another. 'I go along with it, although I rarely feel like it.'

Personally, I supported wholeheartedly—as I'm sure Arndt did too—the right to say no, and have no mean no, and what I read in the book itself did not deny this right. What I read sounded distinctly like compassion. Arndt makes, for example, this comment based on diary feedback from men: 'Many feel duped, disappointed, in despair at finding themselves spending their lives begging for sex from their loved partners. They are stunned to find their needs so totally ignored. It often poured out in a howl of rage and disappointment.'

She quotes one of her diarists who wrote:

I am totally at a loss as to what to do. I do love her and I think she loves me but I cannot live like a monk. I have deliberately tried not to mention sex much at all but now I am so frustrated I don't know what to do. I am at breaking point. I cannot and will not continue on like this. I refuse to go through life begging.

In a chapter entitled 'Fifty thrusts and don't jiggle my book' Arndt writes: 'Yet for men this is usually a private misery. So many men writing to me report that they have never before told anyone about the sexual tension they experience.' She quotes another diarist: 'Over the past several years I have really suffered in silence to the point I could just sit down and cry. I mean, a male my age does not cry, nor does he speak about the problem.'

She explains that women naturally have higher levels of the bonding chemical oxytocin, and that men only experience similar levels during orgasm. Sex is their way to achieve an emotional connection; as one of her sex-deprived diarists wrote: 'I just feel so lonely'. Using diary excerpts, Arndt demonstrates that men want to be wanted; they need to feel like they are capable of giving their partner pleasure; they crave an intimacy with their partner they cannot find in male relationships; and their identity as a man is threatened by a substandard sex life.

Although the media portrayed Arndt as sympathetic primarily to the male side of the story, the book itself did not dismiss the difficulties of women. She presented their side of the conundrum with, to my mind, equal amounts of compassion. As a sex therapist, Arndt has definitely heard both sides and understands the complexity and diversity of sex lives. She does not suggest, for example, all women suffer from low libido: in ten out of her 98 couples the woman was a 'juicy tomato' loving her sex life. Neither does Arndt suggest we endure sex with husbands who behave appallingly. One interesting finding she discusses is that for many of her diarists some of the greatest niggles of their relationships improved automatically if the sex supply reopened and this has been found by other sex therapists as well.

Arndt encourages us to also read a book called *The Sex-starved Marriage: Boosting your marriage libido* by Michele Weiner Davis, a marriage therapist, who first promoted the 'just do it' idea. Michele too expresses compassion, particularly for the spouse being rejected, whether male or female: 'When people believe that their spouses aren't attracted to them, that their marriages or their feelings aren't important, or that an affair is brewing, they feel rejected, suspicious, hurt, resentful, and unloved. They start doubting themselves and their abilities to satisfy their spouses. They often feel deeply depressed about the void in their marriages.'[2]

One reason Weiner Davis believes women should just do it is that it would be 'real giving', which she defines as giving our partners what they value, rather than what we think they should value. She develops the idea of sex as generosity: 'Giving makes you feel good about yourself, it is pleasurable, one gets much back in return as your spouse reciprocates in other areas that may be more important to you'. She concludes: 'When you begin to reap the benefits of bringing back the passion in your marriage, it will leave you wondering, "Why did I wait so long?"'

Both Weiner Davis and Arndt make the point that researchers have challenged the traditional sex response cycle, where desire leads to arousal leads to orgasm. Many women claim they are never, or rarely, in the mood for sex, that they have no desire to get started, yet once it is underway they are capable of 'getting into it'. So arousal can in fact precede desire.[3] This is a major discovery for sex researchers that will lead to a revision of many sex disorders in the bible of psychology, the *Diagnostic and Statistical Manual of Mental Disorders* (the *DSM*). The discovery also suggests that more women could benefit from the 'just do it' approach, rather than waiting indefinitely for desire to spontaneously arise.

PUTTING SEX IN PERSPECTIVE

By teaching us the skill of mindfulness (see the next section for more about this), the Buddha could be hailed as the best sex advisor ever known, but let's not forget the Four Noble Truths. According to the Second Noble Truth, attachment is the cause of suffering and stress. This is no less the case when it comes to sex. If we believe that sex can fix everything, that sex is the answer, that all we need is sex—a message that advertisers ardently hope we will believe in their efforts to sell products that make us feel more sexy—then we can only suffer, as we can never be lastingly satisfied. This might sound like a no-brainer, but when we look at how much effort some of us put into looking sexier, even aside from the rising rates of vaginoplasty and labioplasty (some would add stilettos and brazilians), then we know that some of us may be expecting too much from sex.

Susan Maushart's *Wifework*, though somewhat short on good news, has some down-to-earth advice on sex that resonates with Buddhist teachings in its distrust of 'desire' as the force that should be ruling our lives. Claiming we need to put sex in its proper place, she writes: 'Past the age of raging adolescent hormones, sex doesn't really deserve to reign at the centre of our lives. It's an important driving force in the creation of family life. If we allow it to become the decisive one, its potential for destruction will be assured.'[4]

Her words offer solace to anyone feeling like less than a glowing success in this area of life: 'There is no doubt that the average marriage bed is a highly unerotic space for women, and a somewhat less unerotic space for men. To an extent, that's the nature of the beast. Familiarity, routine, competing needs and stresses all take their toll in time—a remarkably fast time—on marital sexuality.'

Keeping sex exciting, Maushart argues, particularly in the early years of parenting, is one of the greatest challenges of a long-term relationship. Many of us will go through life believing we are abnormally deficient in some way, yet Maushart, and many others including Bettina Arndt, believe having problems in our sex lives is, in fact, the real normal.

•

I've often wondered how much we can blame our culture, which puts out so many messages that undermine our capacity to enjoy sex. Among these are that satisfying sex is:

- for people with good bodies
- for the beautiful
- for the young
- something that only happens at the beginning of a relationship
- something that requires novelty: new partners, new situations
- about orgasms
- a matter of performance, skills, techniques
- reliant on gender stereotypes: alpha males with submissive women
- when men do all the initiating
- demonstrated by pornography.

Perhaps our capacity to enjoy sex is inversely proportional to our belief in these messages. David Schnarch, author of *Passionate Marriage,* seems to think so: 'Most of us aren't ready to differentiate from destructive "normal" beliefs until we're older. Isadora Duncan had it right when she wrote that most of us waste twenty-five or thirty years before we move beyond the conventional sexual lies that permeate society.'[5]

Perhaps good sex has more to do with our capacity for openness and intimacy than a suite of fancy techniques. Schnarch also writes: 'Most people never reach their sexual prime, and those who do, don't reach it until their forties, fifties, and sixties. Profoundly meaningful sex is determined more by personal maturation than physiological reflex. Cellulite and sexual potential are highly correlated.'

If that advice can't give us pause for hope then there's always fine Belgian chocolates.

MINDFULNESS AND SEX

Canadian sex researcher and psychologist Lori Brotto teaches that the missing ingredient in sex is often mindfulness. Lori is at the forefront of the sex research field, in charge of defining the condition 'Hypoactive Sexual Desire Disorder' for the latest revision of the *DSM*.

Lori argues there is a disconnect between the mind of a woman and her body. Her evidence comes from her experiment in which, using a machine called a vaginal photoplethysmograph, she measures the vaginal blood flow of a patient who is watching an erotic video. She almost always finds that the body responds to the video even if the patient herself denies experiencing any response or expresses only distaste for the video. As Lori describes it, a woman's mind swarms all day with details about her children and all the requirements of running a household. It is difficult to switch off this torrent of thoughts, especially for women who add anxious concerns about their appearance, libido or performance. That's why she prescribes so many patients a course of mindfulness.

During her workshops, Lori uses the classic Buddhist exercise of awareness of a raisin. She hands around a container of raisins to the groups of women who attend her workshops and everyone takes one.

The instructions begin: 'I'd like you to start by examining your raisin. Study its shape, its contours, its folds. Touch the raisin with a finger. Look into the valleys and peaks, the highlights and dark crevasses. Lift the raisin to your lips.'

The women place the raisins in their mouths, and she continues: 'Notice where the tongue is, notice the saliva building up in your mouth . . . the trajectory of the flavour as it bursts forth, the flood of saliva, how the flavour changes.'

The raisin exercise trains patients to tune into physical sensation, to fully attend to their present experience, rather than slavishly follow distracting thoughts.

She encourages her patients to practise mindfulness throughout selected daily activities, such as washing the dishes. While most of us have dishwashers these days, every Buddhist book you pick up uses the example of washing the dishes and Brotto is loyal to that example, advising us to notice the smell of the soap suds, the temperature of the water, the colours before our eyes. I guess we can apply the instructions to washing all those saucepans and frying pans that don't fit in the dishwasher. Still, any activity we engage in sends a range of sensory input to the brain. So too in sex, we can ground ourselves in the present by focusing on sensation, by coming back to the physical body in the present, by feeling our own skin and our partner's and opening to the sensory detail.

In Zen Buddhism, practitioners aim to suspend all their prejudices and meet the present moment as if for the first time, with a beginner's mind. We know when we travel to a new place our senses are alert as we pay attention to every detail, eager to take it all in. We find ourselves curious, spontaneous, absorbed, playful even. Yet we do not need to travel to a new place to gain access to such an open, receptive state of mind. We can simply choose to apply 'beginner's mind' to any activity—driving a car, talking to a neighbour, raking some leaves, or to sex.

Some experts emphasise that any focus on the present needs to include our partner. David Schnarch, author of *Passionate Marriage,* names the 'focus on what your body is feeling' that many sex therapists prescribe as responsible for an erosion of sexual intimacy. For Schnarch, 'hot sex' comes from connecting deeply with a partner and he argues that focusing on your own bodily sensations often leads us to tune out our partner, who becomes a potential distraction. He believes that focusing on the sensations of our body can be a way to avoid emotional contact with our partner. At worst, he argues, this approach can leave partners feeling ignored or used.

I'm thinking: do they have to be mutually exclusive? How about trying to focus on both—sensations *and* our partner? Or whichever one helps the most. Then again, for some, either of these options might feel like too tall an order. As one jaded friend said to me: 'I don't want to think about the present moment. Nor do I want to focus on my partner. If I can't go off into fantasies of my own choosing, I don't have a hope of enjoying sex!' Each to their own.

•

When it comes to mindful sex, I did like this quotation that I found on the website of Geoff Dawson, my couples therapist: 'Despite the way sex is abused and sensationalised, it is for the most part a harmless pleasure between consenting adults. At its best sex is both playful and intense and breaks through the tedium of the discursive and ruminating mind into the aliveness of the present moment.'

THINGS TO CONTEMPLATE . . .

• Could other areas of my relationship improve if I valued the role
  of sex in our relationship more highly?

THINGS TO DO

• Take time to consider your partner's point of view when it comes
  to sex.
• Understand that sexual problems in long-term relationships are
  perfectly normal.
• Explore the potential to let go of any culturally driven assumptions
  about sex.
• Try applying the practice of mindfulness in the bedroom as a way
  to let go of the distracted mind. Experiment with 'beginner's mind'
  in bed.
• Don't judge yourself harshly if you feel hesitant about trying a
  mindful approach.

CHAPTER 11

infidelity

ONE IN FIVE WIVES and one in three husbands have been unfaithful to their partner—that's according to the findings of a compilation of 47 different studies involving more than 58,000 respondents, mainly in the United States.[1] While I see little evidence for such high rates of adultery in my own social circles, I once visited a friend who had moved interstate and she assured me it was all happening there. Maybe it occurs in clusters. We could safely assume that the Buddha would have discouraged us from acts of infidelity given he chose to include 'abstaining from sexual misconduct' among his five precepts for lay practitioners (which also include abstaining from taking life, taking what is not given, false speech and intoxicants that lead to carelessness).

Imagining we can find lasting happiness in the arms of another takes us to the land of illusions. Quite apart from the potential for hurting our current partner and children and threatening the stability of a precious family unit—probably two—our experience is unlikely to meet our hopes and expectations. While infidelity is a quest for satisfaction, any found is likely to be short-lived. One reason for this is that the satisfaction is mainly mere relief from the restless state of desire. Then, from a fleeting moment of satisfaction, other desires arise—desires to repeat the experience, to atone for it, to control the numerous consequences—all of which increase the potential for *dukkha*, or stress.

Not that I can't imagine a single situation where sex outside marriage might be worthwhile. While Buddhism is highly focused on ethics and non-harming, that does not make it rigid and inflexible. I have read, for example, in the autobiography of a prominent and highly respected Buddhist scholar from the United States how she and her husband engaged in a sexually open marriage that seemed to hurt nobody and never threatened the strength of their marriage. I believe them. In the writer's view, true love is not possessive; each partner wants the other to be happy, no matter with who.

English monk Ajahn Brahm, who lives in Western Australia, facetiously cites the perfect example of Buddhist non-attachment: your best friend and your partner fall in love and run away together and you feel glad that two people you love so much have managed to achieve greater happiness. That would be true love, he argues.

Alas, very few couples can survive open marriages emotionally unscathed and it would be safe to generalise—and studies from around the world support the generalisation—that most of us see infidelity as the ultimate betrayal. The risk of giving an innocent partner an incurable sexually transmitted disease might be another disincentive.

SEXUAL PREOCCUPATION

Moira (not her real name) is a mother who does not recommend extramarital crushes as a way out of suffering. Here is her story:

> I was very unhappy with my marital relationship, which was dominated by conflict and constant irritability with each other and I started developing crushes on other men. For a while I regularly changed the man I fantasized about, but eventually I settled on one, encouraged by evidence that he was attracted to me. On first discovering that he was interested in me I felt elation. To be found attractive again by someone I found appealing seemed like the ultimate compliment and restored the self-esteem I had lost in my deteriorating marriage.
>
> Every time we ran into each other I felt more sure of his interest in me. I can't tell you how exhilarated this made me feel. Of course, he was married too but I managed to convince myself, based on flimsy evidence, that his wife was not a nice person. Before long I was fantasizing about this man constantly, and I

mean constantly. I imagined scenarios where we could be alone to savour all the joy of cherishing each other, kissing, laughing, making love and feeling close. My fantasies became my refuge. They must have released some chemicals in my brain that made me feel relaxed and even quite blissful. Around the same time I was trying to adopt Buddhist principles for my life—be mindful, compassionate, patient—but it was a losing battle. I could not be mindful and lost in fantasy at the same time.

I soon sensed that my fantasies had become a drug: they made me feel good, they relaxed me, but I was losing control of them. I lost the power to turn them off and they interfered with my ability to concentrate throughout the day—even when other people were talking to me. I was obsessed. I eventually became quite panicked. I knew that enough was enough, that my escape into a fantasy world had gone too far and it was time to come back to reality, but the fantasies had taken over. How would I ever stop them? Again, my self-esteem went down as I imagined myself the only mother with such an out-of-control obsession. At the same time, I was learning that his wife was in fact a good person who had noticed, and felt hurt by, the flirtation. I arranged my life so that I would not run into the man and eventually I found another man to develop a crush on.

With this new man things came to a head and one day we found ourselves in privacy. A passionate 'session' began and within no time we were on the point of removing our clothes. It then transpired that we each had different expectations of what this physical encounter should include, we wanted to move in two conflicting directions. This was an impasse. I paused to collect myself and it struck me that I had not really been enjoying the physical contact at all. I had felt tense and it had been nothing like my fantasies and more like we were characters in a really bad film. I called a halt right there and to my surprise he seemed to agree that this wasn't going to work. From that day, I saw clearly that my fantasies were all illusions. They had led me way, way astray. No experience in the real world would ever live up to them. I was finally cured.

I won my mind back. No longer was it running reel-to-reel fantasies. The problem was: I also lost my drug. Now that I could no longer escape into a fantasy world I was left to feel all the emotions I had avoided. I spent more time angry and eventually felt depressed. I would have to build myself up again from scratch: I would have to commit more to my Buddhist practice, be more mindful of my thoughts and address my marital issues rather than allow conflict to dominate. I sought professional help. My marriage began to improve and even, eventually, underwent a revival.

It is worth taking the Buddha's advice and guarding our thoughts, so that they do not run riot as they did for Moira. When we watch them, we notice how repetitive and circular they can be. How easy it is to become imprisoned by an obsession, romantic or otherwise.

Since Moira presented her escape into fantasies as an addiction, I told her what I had learnt from my volunteer work at Family Drug Support, the phone helpline for families coping with a member who abuses drugs or alcohol that I mentioned in Chapter 7. Those who suffer from substance abuse over many years lose opportunities to learn how to deal with unpleasant emotions. Whereas life forces most people to find ways to deal with anger, sadness, or frustration, those who become dependent on drugs or alcohol can use these to numb any pain. One of the many problems they face upon giving up is that they may never have learnt other ways to cope with unpleasant emotions. The substance has stunted their emotional development.

Moira's experience sounded similar: rather than deal with her anger, disappointment and sadness in her marriage she escaped into a fantasy world so that when she finally let go of that crutch, the problems came crashing down on her, and it took her time to discover tools to deal with them.

ALTERNATIVES TO AN AFFAIR

A couple relationship can be a lonely place for some, a place where basic needs for intimacy and affection go unmet. In most couple relationships, however, progress is possible: in the first chapter I quoted the results of a study that found two-thirds of 'unhappily' married couples described themselves as happily married five years later. Professional help is a possibility, but so is doing our own research and reflecting on different strategies for addressing our problems. For some of us, our fantasies of others might suggest what is missing from our relationship and from there we can try to imagine ways to create whatever we feel we lack. In his book *The Passionate Buddha*, Tibetan Buddhist Robert Sachs includes a chapter called 'The Seduction of Infidelity'. He suggests that if members of the opposite sex do excite us with their attention, we 'go home and create it in our own reality with our Beloved'.

If our relationship feels dull, we might ask ourselves what it would take to re-enliven it. Sachs suggests one potential problem worth investigating: 'If we assume that we know all there is to know about our partner and how far our relationship can take us, the bliss we seek will always elude us. As soon as we think we know our partner, we have already begun to kill our intimacy.'

Sachs also challenges us to question where we habitually search for bliss and reminds us of our inherently loving nature. We yearn for the bliss that is, in fact, our nature and our birthright, and we can experience it when we live with openness. We might experience a small hint of what feels like bliss by extramarital flirting but Sachs explains: 'Then we confuse the bliss with whatever we did to experience it. If we felt that spark in an encounter with someone new, we pursue that person or similar encounters to ensure the same result . . . Bliss is not out there. It doesn't arise because of someone else. Its source is our inherent loving nature.'[2]

We need to recognise that the source of happiness is within us and learn to get in touch with it. Why limit our experience of bliss to sexual relationships, which are inherently unstable? In our culture, we are taught to seek so many positive feelings from sexual or romantic relationships when there are plenty of other more reliable sources of joy and connection. Buddhist teachings, with their emphasis on impermanence, suggest it is deluded to expect one person to make us happy in a lasting way, let alone a relationship based on desire.

My favourite book title would have to be *Wherever You Go, There You Are*, by Jon Kabat-Zinn.[3] We might change our partner, but we take with us into any new relationship all our habitual patterns of thinking and responding. The First Noble Truth, that there is suffering and unsatisfactoriness, would follow us into any new situation. The Buddha taught that we can never set our lives up to be perfect and pain-free. This might sound obvious yet we spend so much mental energy trying to set up, or somehow escape into, just such a life.

Sachs concludes: 'Not being able to escape our own lives, we need to be willing to fearlessly look at what we do to kill the moment, to deaden ourselves to the experience of aliveness with the ones we love.'

TURNING MINDFULNESS ON OUR SEXUAL DESIRE

When we watch the arising of desires, sexual or otherwise, we see the great majority of desires are contradictory, irrational and definitely not worth acting on. Mindfulness of the constant and unrelenting arising of desires helps us to take them less seriously—they are thought bubbles to observe, manage, but rarely act on.

When we are not mindful of desires and their often misleading nature, we are in danger of taking them as orders, or instructions, and we end up in trouble: eating too much, binge drinking, speaking insensitively, flirting with the wrong people, damaging relationships and neglecting higher-order goals or what is important to us.

Mindfulness, focused upon our desires, can help us realise what might lie beneath our sexual fantasies. In his book *The Wise Heart*, Buddhist teacher Jack Kornfield describes his experience as a young monk meditating daily in Thailand:

> Since my vows included celibacy, I had to wrestle with much stronger desires, especially powerful sexual fantasies. I was a young man, and I tried to notice these natural desires mindfully. But they kept returning with great energy. Because they were so strong, my teacher had me pay close attention to the states that came with the fantasy. He especially wanted me to notice how they arose. To my surprise, I discovered that preceding most of these fantasies were feelings of loneliness. I have always had difficulty with loneliness. I am a twin and I suspect that I didn't even want to be alone in the womb. Accepting the loneliness was hard, but my teacher insisted I stay with it. As I explored the loneliness, I found insecurity and a needy kind of emptiness. I remembered these feelings from my early childhood. Much of my sexual desire was an unconscious attempt to fill the emptiness and loneliness. When I held these feelings with compassion, the loneliness began to subside. Gradually I became able to see the fantasies come and go with more mindfulness. In place of only longing, I started to rest in mindfulness, to belong to myself and to the world.[4]

Many respond to sexual fantasies with guilt, shame or a panic to suppress them. Jack Kornfield's experience suggests a potential to approach them with mindful curiosity and learn from them more about what is truly going on inside us.

THINGS TO CONTEMPLATE . . .

- Do I escape into fantasies to avoid dealing with issues at hand?
- To borrow Sachs' words, what do I do to deaden myself to the experience of aliveness with the ones I love?
- Do my sexual fantasies mask an underlying issue such as loneliness, emptiness, insecurity?

THINGS TO DO

- Realise that you will take many of your old problems into any new relationship: wherever you go, there you are.
- Pay attention to your fantasies to discover what might be missing in your relationship. Affection, novelty, adventure, conversation, laughter?
- Take the arising of desires, sexual or otherwise, with a massive grain of salt: desires are constant, contradictory and often self-sabotaging.

CHAPTER 12

tolerance of difficult behaviour

ONE DAY I FOUND myself thinking, if I had three wishes . . . and was surprised at the thought that popped into my mind: *I wish I didn't have to be affected by the moods of others. What freedom that would give me.* And then, 'Why can I not simply be like this?' I don't have to let others' moods affect me and yet I do. If Tomek, or any other member of my family, or even anyone in my vicinity, is in a bad mood I instantly soak it up and make it my own. If anyone feels ill or uncomfortable, I seem to make it my problem and can't relax until they feel better. Now, I could flatter myself and call this empathy, and perhaps to some extent it is, but I suspected something less healthy was going on. I decided to run this one by Geoff.

'If you take your issue to its extreme,' Geoff began, 'and consider marriages where one person has depression, you often find the unde-pressed partner becoming depressed too. They feel like their partner's mood is directed at them, when it isn't. Before long the relationship can be in trouble.'

'Yes, I guess in our self-centredness, we assume that anything our partner feels has to be the result of me, and me alone. There's a tendency to take our partner's mood personally,' I said.

'What can help with those suffering from depression is to warn their partner as soon as they see them, "Look I'm in a really crappy mood today, but it's nothing to do with you." This saves the partner who is not depressed from a lot of speculation and paranoia and can also pave the way for feelings of compassion and concern. But this is also a good idea for couples where neither partner has depression: we can all take responsibility for a bad mood and gently warn our partner that we feel exhausted, or ill, or whatever and advise them to not take our mood personally.'

'So I guess I can encourage a family practice of announcing how we feel so that nobody takes each other's moods personally,' I suggested.

'But what if they are in a bad mood and being personal about it and blaming or nit-picking at you?'

'In some cases you definitely need to be assertive and tell them how their behaviour affects you. But remember, love is a package of four components,' Geoff said, referring to the Buddhist teaching of the Four Divine Abodes. 'If one of the four components is missing then your love will be compromised. In your case, equanimity might be the missing component?'

I brought the Four Divine Abodes to mind and tried to apply them to the partner relationship. We need to cultivate lovingkindness, sometimes defined as friendliness; compassion for our partner's suffering; sympathetic joy for our partner's happiness; and finally the quality of equanimity. Equanimity refers to a calm kind of love encompassing non-attachment to whatever is happening in the relationship right now. It is a less conditional kind of love, dispassionate even, in that it is not vulnerable to extreme highs and lows in the relationship.

Geoff suggested I may be too 'fused' in my relationships and that I needed to become more 'differentiated'. While Buddhist teachings emphasise interdependence, oneness and the delusion of separation, we also need to be able to stand alone, whole and strong in ourselves, in order to be psychologically healthy.

'Isn't that a bit contradictory?' I asked. 'We need to drop the illusion of a separate self and yet we need to be able to differentiate ourselves and avoid fusing with others.'

'In Zen, there's a saying we can apply to any couple, "Not one, not two". We are interdependent but at the same time complete on our own. Have you heard of Indra's net?' asked Geoff.

'Vaguely.' I searched my memory. Indra was some great Indian God living in some heavenly abode where some vast net was strung up.

'At each crossing point in the net there is a jewel,' Geoff reminded me. 'Each individual jewel reflects all the other jewels in the net, like mirrors reflecting images ad infinitum. So each jewel is an individual but at the same time intimately connected with all other jewels: a change in one means a change, however subtle, in every other jewel.'

'So given I am just one jewel I can cultivate non-attachment to the moods of other jewels. Their moods will definitely affect me, as we are all part of the one net, but they needn't overwhelm me because I also stand alone, complete in myself.'

I found further solace from the words of Professor Julie Fitness from Macquarie University. Drawing on five other papers, she offers this analysis that suggests I might not be the only woman doing what she refers to as 'emotion work':

> One interesting aspect of positive family climates concerns the role of women in creating and maintaining them. Some researchers have argued that women still do the bulk of nurturing 'emotion work' in the family by supporting and meeting the emotional needs of their spouses and children. Studies of emotional transmission in the family have demonstrated the existence of an emotional hierarchy, with men's emotions having the most impact on family members overall. This implies that, although the family is a communal context in which family members feel mutually responsible for meeting each other's needs, it is women who feel most responsible for meeting the needs of their spouses and children. Thus, women's emotional expressions tend to revolve around empathic responding to other's needs, while men's emotional expressions tend to be associated with asserting their dominance in the family.[1]

These words helped me to feel more normal in my tendency to take others' emotions on board. Fitness goes on to describe, based on her

research, the responsibility women feel to act as peacekeepers or concili-
ators who help safeguard the quality of father–child relationships.

ACCOMMODATION

Throughout the years of my marriage I have insisted that Tomek never
address me in an angry, impatient tone. If he does, the horse bolts,
and before I know it, I feel wronged, indignant, a victim of the worst
injustice and I snipe back with equal, or surpassing, fury. Should I
hear feedback such as, 'Why do you let the kids/dogs/yourself trash
the house?', I have always practised zero tolerance. Not only have I felt
morally justified in doing so, but I always imagined that zero tolerance
was a logical and effective response that might eventually stamp out
insensitive remarks for all time. Besides, I had to show our sons that
women were strong and capable of standing up for themselves.

Only recently have I paused to question my approach, having
learned that zero tolerance is, evidently, not what people practise
in relationships where marital satisfaction is high. Rather, those in
happy marriages practise what respected researcher Caryl Rusbult calls
'accommodation', where they inhibit the impulse to respond destruc-
tively to unpleasant behaviour and, rather, respond in a conciliatory
manner that reduces tension. Rusbult found that accommodation
was practised among spouses more committed to their marriage. She
also found that those less likely to practise accommodation were more
likely to feel tempted by other potential partners.[2]

The word 'doormat' did spring—okay, surge—to mind when I
first heard of the concept but accommodation is not about letting
people 'get away with it', but about actively trying to resolve problems
while remaining calm. Rusbult describes it as a 'transformation of
motivation', a conscious choice to respond constructively rather than

feed conflict. I could certainly see it had the potential to avoid tit-for-tat mud-slinging, or what the psychological literature calls 'negative escalation spirals', which are characteristic of less happy marriages. I can see now that my former 'zero tolerance policy' turned me into a highly defensive person, complete with an exaggerated sense of self to defend at all costs and a gargantuan sense of separation between Tomek and me.

In Buddhist terms, accommodation can be seen as the Second Noble Truth: desire is the cause of suffering, therefore, let go. Let go of the desire to be right, the desire to retaliate, the desire to defend the 'self', or the strange and self-defeating desire to cling to destructive emotions. Shantideva, an eighth-century Buddhist scholar, suggested we have a choice: we can either remove all the thorns from the surface of the entire world, or wear shoes. That is, I can change Tomek and all the other people who irritate me (impossible), or I can work on changing my own mind (possible).

Happier couples practise accommodation not by suppressing their emotional reaction but by 'reappraising' the offence, or working with their interpretation. In my case, my husband has a high-pressure, demanding job with many unenviable tasks such as meeting deadlines, retrenching people, chasing payment from those who only cough up when threatened with court action, negotiating contracts with the hard-nosed, and confronting non-performers. He does not drink, carouse or resort to physical violence. He has to cope with potential volcanoes of stress and inner tension yet lacks time to pursue much in the way of stress release. How realistic is it for me to expect a smiling saint to arrive on my doorstep every night? Could I not occasionally cut him some slack, as I hope he will do for me on a bad day? The fact remains that, overall, he has a stupendous capacity to cope with pressure and I know that I could not withstand such pressures myself.

We can spend many hours analysing a partner's outburst: *Who is right?* and *What gives him the right to behave that way?* and *Why should I have to put up with it?* and *How can I stop their behaviour?* One of the most generous gifts we can give our partner is some space to lose it from time to time. If outbursts are only occasional and not representative of the usual state of the relationship, then maybe we can afford this. If we can meet their outburst with calm and compassion it is unlikely to last as long as if we jump in and join them, matching their unpleasantness. If we can practise meeting their mood with calm and listen without making judgements, we may find this soothes them and reminds them of a wiser way to be. After all, many of us will need the favour reciprocated within a short time. We are all in the same boat: the demands of modern life can become overwhelming at times. It is normal for most of us, on the odd day, to reach a breaking point and snap. We sometimes need to let go of our expectations and allow our partner to be just another fallible human.

If, despite our best efforts to be calm, patient and loving, our partner continues to lose it a little too often we still have options available to us that fit within the definition of accommodation. We can still provide a calm and constructive response, springing from a sense of commitment. For me, writing a letter to Tomek has been effective, especially if the letter expresses some understanding of Tomek's situation or acknowledges his positive qualities. More on letters in Chapter 15.

ACCOMMODATION FAILURE

If we fail, on occasion, to implement the accommodation approach described above and respond to a perceived offence with rage, then it may not be as catastrophic as it feels at the time. Psychologists have found that, on rare occasions, after tumult and upheaval there can be 'structural improvement' where partners change and grow and begin to perceive each other more realistically.[3] I believe Tomek and I have experienced structural improvement on more than one occasion but my comments would be that for us the road to such improvement felt risky and dangerous to marital stability and that there has to be an easier way. The gains occurred after considerable anguish and in future, when rocky patches arise, I hope to choose wiser, more 'Buddhist' approaches.

Friends from my Buddhist group, Anna and Arthur, are the parents of two young children and Anna felt challenged by what she describes in her personal diary as 'the sheer demanding, grinding nature of being a full time mum—the total 24/7 responsibility—and the lack of any status I receive'. Anna and Arthur have experienced structural improvement, due to their eventual willingness to let go of strong anger and open up to the relief of forgiveness. Anna described their experience:

> Our worst fight ever involved a huge rush of anger coming up in both of us, and ended in us just screaming at each other. No words—just making a loud noise—quite spectacular! Basically it was about me feeling dissatisfied with the split of domestic and paid work in the marriage along with my issues about 'what to do with my career'. This makes me moody, which makes Arthur moody, and we eventually had to let the pressure out.
>
> I slept in my son Sam's room that night. In the morning I didn't know what would happen. I had worked myself up into such a state I thought the relationship was over and we would have to divorce. I lay on the mattress in Sam's room wondering what to do next and dreading having to talk to Arthur. I still believed I'd have to leave with the boys.

I couldn't quite muster the original anger at Arthur and was feeling waves of sheepishness. Then, the door slowly opened and Arthur came in with a cup of tea for me. He had a sheepish smile too and sat down on the bed and just said something like, 'What are we going to do now?' or 'I don't like fighting with you, I love you'. They are the usual things he says. I had a brief moment of trying to take the moral high ground and stay angry, but this was quickly pushed away by an overwhelming desire to be friends again and hug. And that is what we did. And it felt really good.

So nothing was resolved at this point with regard to the hundred little stresses within our relationship. But it was nonetheless such a healing moment because he came back to me and forgave me—and I him. It suddenly became crystal clear that I loved him and I didn't want to be without him. I found the whole thing very cleansing, healing and confirming of our relationship. It moved us out of a rut. The fight made both of us face some problems in the relationship and we have slowly, over the weeks, made changes to how we do things around the house.

Anna sent me copies of the weekly timetables and house cleaning lists that evolved following their fight, assuring me that they were working well.

Yes, on occasion, tumult can lead to improvement. The key to surviving the storm seems to be an ability to eventually let go of attachments—to grudges, to being right, to righteous anger—and to open ourselves to love and compassion for our partner.

One of the dysfunctional beliefs I mentioned in Chapter 3 was that those in good relationships experience no conflict. Research has found strong evidence that conflict is no predictor of divorce and that failure to address issues is far more dangerous to a relationship.

That said, we need to engage in conflict in skilful ways and keep in mind that what is said is not nearly as important as how it is said.

THE SURRENDERED WIFE

Years ago I read about a book that had suddenly found a cult following called *The Surrendered Wife*. I was appalled at the title: obviously some traditionalist was trying to undo all the hard work of the feminist sisterhood by just giving in to male domination. Years later, after learning about the concept of accommodation, I borrowed the book from my library. I wondered if maybe the conciliatory, calm and constructive approach of accommodation was what the author had meant by the word 'surrendered'.

The author, Laura Doyle, far from being a subservient defeatist turned out to be a high-powered career woman who felt constantly frustrated at what she perceived as her husband's incompetence. She was a self-described 'controlling wife', nit-picking, criticising and nagging, which only seemed to alienate her husband. For her, surrender was about learning to trust in her husband's capacity to help run the household and to leave him be. She eventually decided to let him do things his own way and was amazed to find that this approach rekindled all the lost intimacy and connection. They were like young lovers again. She decided that control and intimacy were opposites. 'As I stopped bossing him around, giving him advice, burying him in lists of chores to do, criticizing his ideas and taking over every situation as if he couldn't handle it, something magical happened. The union I dreamed of appeared. The man who wooed me was back.'[4]

Her book struck a chord with thousands. She started running surrendered wife meetings, then workshops, then lectures and a collaborative website. Although she was by no means a Buddhist author, Laura's surrendering can be seen as the letting go of attachments. She decided to let go of doing things her way, of her ideas about 'the right and only way to do things'. She decided, instead, to turn inward. 'To remind myself of my new priorities, I adopted the word "surrender" as my mantra, because it was shorter and more to the point than saying, "stop trying to control everything". I repeated "surrender" to myself silently over and over again.'

Unfortunately, Doyle took the idea of surrender way too far for the average self-respecting woman. Later in the book she advised us to say, 'whatever you think' to our husband's every suggestion. I like to think that all but the most insecure husbands would find such a wife, pretending to have no mind of her own, plain annoying. Tomek, with his penchant for robust debate, certainly would.

Throughout her book Doyle assumed that all wives were like her: controlling. Yet in my own relationship it was the reverse: if anyone was controlling it was Tomek. I cast my mind back over all the mothers I'd met. Were they all controlling? Some possibly were, plenty weren't, but one thing was sure: most wives I'd met wished their husband shared the load more when it came to housework.

I have had the odd friend over the years who has described herself as controlling. Since I know how it feels to be picked at over my house-keeping skills I have asked these friends: 'If you so want him to contribute more around the house, why would you find fault with the way he does it? Surely that just gives him the right to say, "Fine, do it yourself."' As I've always said to Tomek, 'Surely, all that matters is that the job gets done to a decent standard, rather than exactly how.' (I've managed to solve the problem of feeling controlled by permanently banning Tomek from the kitchen when I cook and refusing to accept him as a passenger when I drive.)

One friend married to a landscaper countered with, 'It's just that he spends all day working to the highest standards creating perfectly manicured gardens. It seems insulting that he comes home to his supposed loved ones and just drops all that care and eye for detail.' I suppose if our partner is doing a glaringly poor job it might be worth holding them to account if the task is important. Letting the children go to bed in their day clothes with unbrushed teeth, for example, could be worth addressing. Methods of hanging the laundry and packing the dishwasher—not so much.

THINGS TO CONTEMPLATE . . .

- Can I understand that I am both fully whole on my own, yet at the same time inextricably connected to every other being? 'Not one, not two.'
- Do I feel fully committed to my partner? Would being more committed help me to respond to aggravations in a calmer and more conciliatory way, as the research suggests?
- Do I work with my own mind, cultivating patience and tolerance or do I madly try and squash every irritation that comes my way in a never-ending quest?

THINGS TO DO

- When you feel angry with your partner, try reappraising the offence. There is always more than one possible interpretation or emphasis.
- Practise generosity by allowing your partner some space to lose it occasionally, to be another fallible human being.
- Take heart that sometimes after fierce conflict, improvements can occur.

- Don't avoid conflict, but do manage it wisely. Calm and conciliatory is best, if possible.
- Let go of some of your high standards if they make you too controlling. Try a little 'surrender'.

CHAPTER 13

forgiveness and understanding

GIVEN THE INEVITABILITY OF conflict in a long-term relationship it is highly necessary to cultivate the capacity to forgive. Grudge-holding kills off any potential for marital satisfaction. As Michele Weiner Davis, author of *The Sex-starved Marriage,* writes, 'In my years as a marriage therapist, I can tell you with confidence that holding grudges is one of the most effective methods for killing desire that I've ever seen.'[1] If we hold onto the bad feelings from every conflict we experience, what kind of person will we turn into? In Buddhist terms, grudge-holding is detrimental to our karma. While forgiveness feels like an act of kindness to another, it is equally an act of compassion towards ourselves, as we free up mental space for more nourishing material than our grudge. Grudge-holding punishes the grudge-holder so many times more than it does the offending partner.

Forgiveness is about letting go of the past and studies support the notion that forgiving is one of the best things you can do for your wellbeing, your relationship, and even your health. In her book *Lovingkindness*, Sharon Salzberg, a meditation teacher of world renown, writes: 'In some ways to be able to forgive, to let go, is a type of dying. It is the ability to say, "I am not that person anymore, and you are not that person anymore." Forgiveness allows us to recapture some part of ourselves that we left behind in bondage to a past event.'[2]

What helps us to forgive? The psychological research lists a few ingredients: empathy, reluctance to engage in rumination, letting go of anger and resentment, the ability to admit that you too are capable of lapses, and commitment to a relationship.

It was time for another confession to Geoff.

'I don't think I'm very good at forgiving,' I admitted. 'In fact, if you asked me to write a list of the five meanest things Tomek has done to me, I don't think I'd even have to pause to scratch my head. I could write that list straight away!'

Geoff did not look alarmed. He looked amused. 'What people often don't realise about forgiveness,' he offered, 'is that it's a process. A process with several stages.'

This was a good start. Maybe I had just been overlooking a step or two.

'People who are trying to be spiritual or even just nice and good,' Geoff continued, 'might practise that thing I mentioned to you last week called "spiritual bypassing" and try to go straight to forgiveness because they see this as more "Buddhist". But they are often skipping important steps.'

'I think I may have been guilty of that,' I admitted. 'In the past I have congratulated myself for being such a forgiving person. Tomek and I seemed to be interacting amicably despite some earlier offence. Yet if he so much as took my hand, my body knew the truth, and I would pull away. So I had not really forgiven him at the deepest level. So what are these steps?'

'Well, the first thing to accept and really tune into is how much you *don't* want to forgive,' Geoff smiled. 'That needs to be acknowledged and accepted without beating yourself up for it.'

'Yeah, I guess there's no point pretending forgiveness is easy or fast,' I added.

'Then we need to be with all the painful emotions that emerge in response to the other person's behaviour. We need to open to the sadness, disappointment, fear, or feelings of betrayal. We need to experience these emotions fully and let them run their course before we can let them go.'

'Is forgiveness always the way to go? Do you think Buddhists and other religions can be a bit fundamentalist about forgiveness? I mean, surely, there are some actions, perhaps repeated actions or situations where a partner shows no remorse, that it would possibly be stupid to forgive.'

'Sure. Buddhism is never about blanket rules that apply in every situation such as "we must always forgive",' answered Geoff.

'I can imagine,' I suggested, 'that the human reluctance to forgive may have even helped us to survive. It may have been dangerous at certain points in history to forgive, say, all those marauding hordes invading the villages.'

'We often get confused about the definition of forgiveness,' Geoff reflected. 'It doesn't mean that if someone has treated us abusively we need to feel friendly towards them. You can, for example, forgive someone but stop seeing them altogether.'

Our conversation seemed to be wandering away from the context of couples with children who don't have the option of suddenly ceasing contact, so I asked Geoff, 'What advice do you usually give the couples you see on the topic of forgiveness?'

'I think the most important thing to know is the power of apology. If both partners can just be capable of saying sorry, then there is always the potential for relationship repair.'

I knew Geoff was right and am proud to say that this is something my whole family excel at. Apologies are part of our daily life, and need to be. I find I can be consumed with despair over some marital spat with Tomek but if he just says a simple, heartfelt 'sorry', my despondency lifts immediately. Sometimes I have followed him around the house begging to hear the word so that I can be released from the painful emotions. And it's amazing how immediate is the effect. Instant relief.

I still had some outstanding forgiveness issues to explore with Geoff however, so I pressed on.

'What I find really hard to forgive are some of the things that Tomek isn't sorry for and I guess there's no reason for him to be sorry. He has some characteristics—and I guess it's similar for most couples—that limit the scope of my life. We are attracted to very different types of hobbies, holidays and people so in compromising, you end up making what feels like huge sacrifices. My desire, say, for a wider social life than we have, to explore different styles of music and food, to try new experiences and a few other heartfelt priorities . . .'

I thought of some other couples I know who felt similarly. A wife gave up reading at night because the lamp kept her husband awake. A husband gave up cycling because his wife complained at being woken at 5 am. Some couples feel torn at the thought of seeing their parents and siblings because their partner can't stand the in-laws. While relationships can open worlds for us, they all eventually involve some closing down of our options, some major sacrifices. These can feel hard to forgive.

'I think what we're talking about here,' Geoff ventured, 'is the need for acceptance. Sometimes we just need to accept our partner for the way they are. We need to find ways to live with that rather than trying to mould them in our image.'

Many Buddhist teachers, including Geoff, borrow the serenity prayer from Christianity, perhaps our best hope for peaceful relationships:

God, grant me the serenity
To accept the things I cannot change,
The courage to change the things I can,
And wisdom to know the difference.

This is the same message as that of Shantideva, mentioned in the last chapter. The world is covered with thorns, thistles and stones. We can go into battle against each individual thorn, thistle and stone, or we can wear shoes. Likewise, rather than change all the annoying people in the world, we can protect ourselves by working on our own minds. If we learn our way around our own mind and learn to manage our thoughts and reactions more skilfully, then we can save ourselves a considerable amount of self-created suffering.

A relatively recent approach in couples therapy, called Integrative Behavioural Couple Therapy (IBCT), differs from traditional therapies by focusing not only on changing problematic behaviours but also on bringing couples to accept some of those inevitable differences that are hard to stamp out. As one psychology website puts it: 'The greatest harm to the couple comes not from the incompatibilities; rather, the greatest harm comes from the rigid, negative, and excessive emotional responses that develop from these unresolved issues.'[3]

According to IBCT, when facing these most intractable differences, couples need to avoid blame and resentment, to listen and cultivate empathy and compassion, to work with their own reactions rather than the perceived faults in their partner.

ACKNOWLEDGING OUR PARTNER'S PAIN

We have established that forgiveness, and the ability to apologise, are vital ingredients for a happy relationship. Another powerful ingredient is the feeling that we understand our partner. Cultivating understanding, after all, makes forgiveness easier but also helps us to change our own mind rather than trying to change everything that annoys us about our partner.

Tomek has ongoing aches and pains from a youth filled with contact sport. This means that on some days he can't participate fully in family life and we might cancel planned outings that involve physical activities. On the days when I forget to be self-aware, I feel exasperated at having to drop our plans. Yet this kneejerk reaction is devoid of compassion for the physical pain he sometimes has to endure for months on end.

It would be comical, if it wasn't so tragic, the way partners can be so frustrated with each other's physical aches, pains and illnesses. How dare he catch the flu when I need him to drive the kids to sport, visit his in-laws and contribute to the household? Some wicked women even refer disparagingly to the phenomenon of 'man-flu'. (Don't laugh!) Humour aside, we can learn to treat such times as a chance to cultivate, and express, compassion. This of course needs to be a reciprocal arrangement so it is worth informing a partner how we too want to be treated when we are ill or aching.

On a good day, we might call to mind the words from the Buddhist lovingkindness meditation: *May you be well. May you be free from suffering.* We might also remember how short-changed we ourselves feel when people respond to our physical pain with impatience or apathy. Believing nobody cares, we can even feel lonely and depressed as we battle to recover our health.

We cultivate compassion for a partner's physical problems, but also for emotional difficulties. Tomek's *dukkha* in life is a different type to mine so it's easy for us to overlook or downplay each other's stress. His *dukkha* comes mainly from constant, unrelenting work pressure and little time to rest and recharge. Most of my *dukkha* comes from job insecurity, worrying about various relationships and self-doubt—all areas he never worries about. We both need to call on our imagination to understand, and provide empathy for, each other's experience of stress.

Although Tomek is not the type to dwell on, or even mention, painful memories, they surely haunt him on some level. As a refugee from a once-troubled country, he has lived through times of insecurity, anxiety and fear and they would have left residual feelings that affect him today in the form of a need for control, comfort, predictability and safety. I don't share such needs to nearly the same degree so I can conveniently forget his background and make demands according to my own needs for novelty, discovery and adventure. The only answer is for both of us to practise acceptance of who the other is and ensure our decisions do not too often favour one party at the expense of the other.

CONSIDER THE CAUSES AND CONDITIONS

How easy it is to demonise our partners by slapping a label on them. Whether the label is 'selfish', 'mean', 'moody' or 'cold', such labels suggest our thinking about our partner has solidified. We have turned them into a fixed object and this ignores all kinds of Buddhist teachings such as impermanence, compassion and karma (the more we think simplistically, the more we'll think simplistically). In order to deepen our insight, the Buddha encourages us to see all phenomena as the result of causes and conditions.

Take my husband Tomek, for example. He has a preoccupation with money that I do not share to anywhere near the same extent and which causes numerous marital issues for us. You may have heard the expression, 'Behind every successful man is a woman who couldn't be more astonished.' In my case, Tomek has achieved some career success and I have indeed been astonished. I am not astonished because I doubt his competence. I am astonished because I have never noticed any strong desire in him to climb a corporate ladder, to wield power over others or even impress others. All I have noticed is his desire to earn money. Climbing the corporate ladder was merely the most effective way to do this.

'People who think money can't buy happiness just don't know the right shops'—or so some of us believe. Tomek would probably rephrase that: 'People who think money can't buy happiness haven't driven the Nissan GTR.'

I could easily brand Tomek with the label 'greedy' but this would turn him into a two-dimensional character, lacking in complexity. It would also give me an excuse to deny him any compassion and understanding. If I consider the causes and conditions behind Tomek's focus on money, then I can understand it and might even say, 'With those experiences, with that family history, I would probably be the same'.

Tomek's life and the life of his family back in Poland has been marked by insecurity and uncertainty. It is hard to deny that money can be a bulwark against such experiences. I often find it helpful to remind myself of his family history.

Tomek's mother, Barbara, was 8 years old when the German army invaded the Ukrainian town where she lived. Like most children in Central Europe during the war years, Barbara and her siblings were often hungry, with most grocery stores bearing signs 'Germans only'. It was Barbara's responsibility to stand guard outside her house while her family listened to the radio news. This was a heavy responsibility for a child: if her family were caught with a radio they would be executed in the town square. The Germans took one of Barbara's older brothers away in a truck to an Austrian concentration camp from where he escaped and spent many months on the run. Barbara's cousins, for the crime of being Polish, were sent to Siberian labour camps, where some were tortured and executed.

At the war's end, the Allies handed several Eastern Bloc countries, among them the Ukraine, into Russian control and Barbara's family joined the subsequent mass exodus into Poland. After a five-week journey in a cattle-train Barbara's family settled in a town full of refugees, among them the man she eventually married. Everybody lived crammed into small, drab apartments in Russian-built high-rise blocks, under the watchful eyes of a communist government. Tomek and his sister grew up with their parents in a tiny one-bedroom unit.

Economic prospects were bleak and, without hope of improvement, most of the men in Tomek's town became alcoholics. Tomek's
father died of cancer aged 52. Barbara, the primary breadwinner,
had qualified as a dentist and worked full-time. They were deemed
a fortunate family since her higher than average income meant they
could afford a car and a telephone. Still, Barbara had to pay 40 per
cent of her income to the government as 'superannuation', although
she never saw the money again.

Tomek qualified as a mechanical engineer but, like many educated
Poles at the time, decided to leave. Along with his Polish girlfriend,
Tomek became a refugee and hitchhiked to Austria where he lived
for eighteen months. To earn money he donated blood plasma so
many times that eventually it was too hard to insert a needle into his
heavily scarred arms. In time, he found work as a carpenter but came
to believe he would never be accepted as an equal among Austrians.
He applied to other countries and was accepted by Australia due to
his engineering qualification. He married his girlfriend so that she
could come too.

Tomek's early years in Australia were difficult. He spoke no English
and worked as an egg-sorter, a factory-worker on night shift, a fridge
mechanic and finally as an engineer. After more than a decade his
marriage ended and Tomek lost the financial nest egg they had built
up together—he was back to zero. Three years later he met me.

In Tomek's view, he has taken large risks for the chance of a
better quality of life than Poland could provide. He has tasted a life
of economic hardship, with no family to fall back on, lost everything
twice, and knows what he wants. He wants money—and the security
it brings. From the comfort of my Sydney upbringing, I do not feel
I can judge him too harshly for that.

I have described causes and conditions from Tomek's environment
for the way he is but there are also genetic causes and conditions

that help explain why people are the way they are. Speaking more generally, we are all born with a certain temperament and a set of predispositions. While our genes do not offer the full explanation for who we are, they are certainly powerful contributors. Many scientists claim that, for any particular personal characteristic, genes account for a third to a half of the reason we are a certain way. Our genetic inheritance might mean that we are especially prone to, say, anger, anxiety, impulsivity, or sadness. Take the example of anxiety. If we have inherited a tendency to be anxious from a parent, then we might be subject to not only the genes for anxiety but also the modelling of anxious behaviour from the anxious parent.

Whether our partner's difficult behaviours have genetic or environmental causes, or both, it is easier to be compassionate if we remember the reasons they are the way they are. If this is difficult, imagine doing it for your own child, and how you would want their future partner to be understanding too. We can always take inspiration from the love we feel for our children and try to send some of this infinite, unconditional goodwill in the direction of our partner.

•

Buddhist psychology divides people into three personality types using the Three Mental Torments: greed, anger and delusion. While we all suffer from all three, each one of us struggles with one more than the other two. In Buddhist terms, Tomek suffers most from greed, while for me greed is the least troublesome: I am far more caught up by delusion, or a tendency to be confused and indecisive.

In fact, I have always been somewhat drawn to the ascetic life. I have never been all that materialistic. I'm not motivated by money and what it can buy me. I try to live by the maxim 'a man is rich according to his needs': that is to say, need little and you are already rich. I aspire to keep my life simple: I avoid shopping and buy most of my clothes in op shops or at community clothes-swap events; I haven't been to a hair salon for about seventeen years; my hobbies are generally cheap. With expensive belongings, I have found, comes tension and worry from the possibility of damage, of wear and tear and breakdown. Did I say 'possibility'? The Buddha's teaching of impermanence would suggest, rather, inevitability.

I have often fantasised about following the example of the character in Tim Winton's classic Australian novel *Cloudstreet,* where the mother of the family moved into a tent in the backyard—just to prove to myself that I am not owned by my belongings or by the material comforts in my life. Due to numerous practical considerations, including damaging the lawn, this will never happen. While greed is not my problem, delusion troubles me the most of the three poisons in that I often find myself vague, forgetful or indecisive. (Well, I *used* to think I was indecisive, but I'm starting to have second thoughts . . .)

With Tomek suffering from 'greed' and me suffering from 'delusion', I guess we could be called a mixed marriage—which may be a good thing. I have often wondered what happens when two 'greedys' marry each other (high levels of debt?), or two 'deludeds' (nothing ever gets done?), or two 'angrys' (lots of walking on eggshells?).

THINGS TO CONTEMPLATE . . .

- Do I hold grudges? If so, what price do I pay for this? Could I afford to let go of my grudges and forgive?
- Do I kid myself that forgiveness is easy? Do I recognise that it may take time and involve several stages?

- Are there characteristics of my partner that I just need to learn to accept? Could I let go of my insistence that my partner change to be more like me, in any particular area?
- Which personality type am I? Greedy, angry or deluded? How about my partner? How does this affect our relationship?

THINGS TO DO

- Apologise when you behave badly. Encourage your partner to do likewise as it makes it so much easier to forgive.
- Be aware of your reactions to your partner's physical pain and try to cultivate compassion.
- Use your imagination to help you feel empathy for a partner's emotional difficulties.
- Keep in mind the causes and conditions— which may derive from nature, nurture or the environment—that give rise to your partner's characteristics. Don't just slap on a label that demonises them, or limits your perception of who they are.

CHAPTER 14

turning things around

THE FIELD OF PSYCHOLOGY has traditionally focused on the negative, as researchers have studied mental illness, psychopathology or what can go wrong in our mental health. More recently, a large proportion of researchers have shifted their focus to studying positive mental health and its causes, starting a movement called 'positive psychology'. So too with this book: up to this point there has been a focus on problems as we've explored topics like anger, conflict, mismatched libidos and difficult behaviours. With these final chapters, I aim to dwell on the positive, to explore ways to be more loving, to deepen our connection with our partner, to look at what works.

We can reach a point in our relationship where we are ripe for change. We may be sick of living in conflict, tired of a habit of bickering, lonely from a lack of communication or eager to liven up a relationship that feels dull. This chapter is about turning things around and will start with some advice from a Buddha-inspired neuroscientist.

TAKING IN THE GOOD

I spoke briefly in the Introduction to this book about the human 'negativity bias', whereby we have evolved to focus far more on negative information than on positive. As the saying goes, we Teflon the positive and Velcro the negative. We sometimes hear actors, for example, claim they can read a hundred good reviews of their latest performance and one critical review but rather than feeling happy, they focus disproportionately on the negative review, and feel devastated. Sadly, in the human mind, bad outweighs good. Of course, taking an evolutionary perspective, this has been adaptive, or useful, throughout human history. Focusing on the negative has helped us to pay attention to danger, helped us to solve problems and motivated us to take action that enabled us to survive. The overly positive types probably died out, eaten alive, as they failed to attend to imminent dangers.

Now that we are no longer surrounded by wild animals or hostile tribes, the negativity bias is a psychological burden and we can choose to stop carrying it. I remember this anecdote by popular English monk Ajahn Brahm, who has a reputation for being humorous and entertaining, if slightly irreverent.

There were two chicken farmers. One entered his chicken coop and proceeded to fill his basket with chicken shit. When he took it into the house, family members asked, 'Why did you bring all that stinking stuff in here? You should have left it outside to turn into fertiliser!' The second chicken farmer entered his chicken coop and proceeded to fill his basket with eggs. His family members said, 'That's great—now we can sell some and even make an omelette.'

What do you bring into your home? Are you a shit-collector or an egg-collector?

He challenged the audience to consider their relationship with their partners too. Do you hold onto all the past hurts and disappointments? We might feel happier if we let go of some of our stinking old complaints and start collecting more eggs.

I have shared the story of the chicken farmers with Tomek and often tease him: 'Are you shit-collecting again?' I have also apologised to him, on occasion, when it is me who is guilty of shit-collecting.

The guru of relationship science, psychologist John Gottman, is especially aware of our negativity bias and its potential to damage our most important relationship. If we want to avoid divorce and stay satisfied with our relationship, he asserts, we need to ensure that for every negative interaction in our marriage there are five positive interactions.[1] This means that we need to offset any incident of nagging, criticising, or temper-flaring, with five incidents of praise, affection, friendliness or laughter.

This five to one ratio is useful to commit to mind: it suggests that if we mistreat our spouse with, say, one little insult, it takes more than one little compliment to offset the impact. The happiest relationships boast a ratio of eight positive interactions for every negative one. Zen teacher Thich Nhat Hanh is quoted by Buddhists of all traditions when he advises us to 'water the seeds of joy' in our minds and the minds of those we live with, rather than the seeds of suffering. 'Selective watering,' he calls it, and the more we water the seeds of joy the more joy we will feel. Cultivation is key.

Yet even if we can achieve this five to one ratio, another problem is that partners fail to notice many of the positive interactions. One study, for example, tracked what behaviours partners noticed over four weeks only to find that both men and women did not notice about a quarter of the positive behaviours their partners engaged in for them.[2] In his brilliant book *Buddha's Brain: The practical neuroscience of happiness, love, and wisdom*, neuropsychologist Rick Hanson raises the bar, recommending that we do more than merely notice any positive actions. He urges us to 'take in the good' on a deep level so that we mould the overall feel of our relationship into something more positive.[3]

Hanson suggests three steps are involved in taking in the good. First we need to 'turn positive facts into positive experiences' by bringing a mindful awareness to any positive facts, no matter how trivial they are. He advised us to open up to them and allow them to affect us rather than becoming distracted by the next pull on our attention. Next, we need to 'savor the experience', staying with it for even 20 seconds. This is more likely to implant the 'good' in our memories. The final step is to picture or sense the experience entering deeply into your mind or body: 'Keep relaxing your body and absorbing the emotions, sensations, and thoughts of the experience.'

Hanson reminds us that it takes an *active* effort to overwrite our natural negativity bias so taking in the good is effectively 'righting a neurological imbalance'. In Hanson's words, 'If you take in positive experiences, then you fill up your own cup and become less dependent on external conditions; in effect, your happiness becomes increasingly unconditional'. This is not to say that we gloss over negative events or suppress negative emotions, nor that we cling or grasp at positive experiences. While we pay attention to any emotional experience that arises, it is sensible and wise to foster, to actively cultivate, emotions that bring us peace and contentment.

Don't trust your memory

We commonly assume that our memories of past events are stored as exact replicas, like video recordings, of what happened. Yet when we compare our memories of an event with somebody else's we can end up arguing over the details of how it unfolded. Within the same family, memories of the past can differ dramatically from person to person. Memory can be particularly unreliable in a couple relationship, not to mention extremely prone to the negativity bias. I've lost count over the number of arguments Tomek and I have had that follow this template:

'But you said *x*!'

'That's not what I said. I said *y*.'

'No. I'm sure you said *x*. That's why I went and did *a, b* and *c*.'

I have even, on one occasion, asked Tomek to sign the notes I typed after one of our discussions, knowing that in a year's time we might not remember what we agreed upon.

I find memory particularly untrustworthy when I feel disappointed or angry with Tomek: I paint our entire past together as misery. Then, when things run smoothly I believe stability to be the norm. It is as though our relationship has a split-personality with neither personality aware of the existence of the other. At one stage, I felt confused: which one was the reality? I decided to give our relationship a mark out of ten every day over an extended period of time. I would graph it and then I would have my answer. In fact, I have engaged in this exercise twice over the course of my marriage only to discover that most of the time we, in fact, live on an even keel. Most of the time, we were stable with marks of seven and eight, punctuated by a couple of bad days every now and then—usually a Saturday, for some reason. Since I struggle to cope with conflict and ill-feeling—not least the insomnia it causes me—I am willing to stay up late into the night to overcome negative feelings rather than spend two weeks not speaking. So the worst times, at least by the time the children had reached school age, have never been too drawn out.

Cognitive scientists describe memory as 'reconstructive'. Every time we access a memory of a particular past event we revise it to suit our current mood or knowledge. It can be difficult to study the histories of people with depression, for example, because they tend to suffer from a depressive bias, remembering large swathes of their past in a negative light. Researchers who looked at eight different studies found that it was possible in 31 per cent of people, taking an average of the results of the eight studies, to 'implant' false memories by using simple devices like false photos and narratives.[4]

When our marriages are going well, we practise rosy retrospection. When relations go awry, the opposite. Researchers studying 373 very happy newlywed couples found those whose marriages had soured two years later had revised those happy newlywed memories to be negative.[5] It is as though we have this need to say: 'I've known the truth all along'. We crave a consistency of perception. The researchers found these results 'frightening', adding, 'Such biases can lead to a dangerous downward spiral. The worse your current view of your partner is, the worse your memories are, which only further confirms your negative attitudes.'

The reconstructive nature of memory is all the more reason to allow time to take in the good. It takes effort to overcome the negativity bias so we need to pause and consolidate positive experiences, committing them to memory and purposely re-running happy memories. This morning I was barking at my sons for their disorganised approach to preparing for school, so we started the day on a sour note. Working at my computer hours later I received a text from my eleven-year-old, Alex: 'I love you so much'. I smiled and returned to my work.

Suddenly I caught myself. 'No! Take a full minute to relax and enjoy this,' I instructed myself. 'Let it sink in so that you will remember its deliciousness over the long term.' I tried to bring the text message to mind several times throughout the day, savouring the pleasant feelings, and it lifted my mood every time.

So too with Tomek. Many tiny but pleasant things happen between us: he might laugh at one of my jokes, give me a quick shoulder massage, listen patiently during my vexed phone calls about the phone company. So many acts we fail to notice, appreciate and remember. Yet we have the option of 'taking them in'. It doesn't take more than a few seconds. It does take a conscious mind state. It is a matter of waking up, or showing up, in the present moment to notice the small gestures of kindness or consideration.

Buddhist friend Danielle found that it was also helpful to 'express the good':

I have developed a habit over many years that I have not brought much awareness to. Whenever I get together with my sister, we grumble about our husbands, trading stories about domestic incompetence, shortcomings in their parenting and failures in their social and relationship skills. We often laugh about it all and commiserate and we have always believed that it makes us feel better. Lately though we have challenged ourselves to express some of the good things our husbands do. We've started adding incidents that we appreciate and I notice that this feels even better, not just during the conversation, but long after too, such as when we are with our husbands later in the day.

I don't think it would be overgeneralising to say that women complain about their partners behind their backs much more than men do. Perhaps this is to be expected given women, in many households, do more than their fair share of the heavy lifting in childcare and housework, if we are to believe the regular reports in the newspaper (and we do).

We don't want to deprive ourselves of a valuable therapy session, an opportunity to vent or laugh, but there are two things to keep in mind if we complain about our partner behind their back. First, we need to remember that any friend we vent with is highly unlikely to challenge our interpretations. The cultural norm is to be supportive—indeed it would sound unsympathetic, even judgemental, to be otherwise. The trouble is that talking to friends who endlessly confirm our every thought can keep us in a rut where we forgo any opportunity to see our situation differently. Then our perceptions can become very solidified and difficult to challenge.

The second risk is that if our confidantes only ever hear about our partners' flaws and mistakes, they develop a skewed view which dooms them to give us feedback that is not based on reality: 'I don't know how you put up with him—I'd just leave'. At worst, they may develop a strong dislike for our partner leading them to avoid him, badmouth him to others, or stop inviting you anywhere as a couple.

Sometimes, on the other hand, women can experience epiphanies upon hearing others complain about their partners and can even find themselves feeling fortunate. They might think to themselves, *Mine is actually the opposite of that*, or, *Thank god I don't have to put up with that*. Caught in the middle of a partner-bashing session, we sometimes find fuel to appreciate our own. We just need to remember to hold those appreciative thoughts, to really 'take them in'.

BIG MIND, SMALL MIND

A helpful distinction Zen Buddhists make is between 'big mind' and 'small mind'. Shunryu Suzuki, founder of the San Francisco Zen Center, likened big mind to the ocean, small mind to the waves. 'Big mind', like the ocean, is limitless, all-inclusive, non-reacting, non-resisting. The waves are part of the ocean but they are fleeting and insubstantial. When it comes to our relationship, we can see thoughts of *my* pain, *my* struggles, as waves that emanate in the small mind, the mind identified with the false notion of a fixed, solid and separate self.

Buddhist practice challenges us to shift into 'big mind', the mind that sees not *my* pain, *my* struggles but instead the universal pain, the universal struggles of which our small mind is but an infinitesimal part. This way we take *my* pain less personally, perceiving it as part of the difficulties of all the deluded beings who struggle with their sense of separation, or as part of a long stream of causes and conditions rather than an isolated event. 'Big mind' is capable of seeing the struggles of 'small mind' and watching its processes. 'Small mind' is constricted, turned in on itself, painful, habit-driven.

With this distinction in mind, I can challenge myself as I interact with Tomek: *Am I operating out of small mind or big mind?* When

I can catch myself caught up in small mind, it is a moment of awakening, and I am able to shake up all that stale energy and let go, or try something new. Tomek and I can be like a couple of lawyers, both wanting the last word, both wanting to win the argument. 'Big mind' knows that there is no such thing as winning the argument: how can either of us say we have won when all we have really achieved is a reinforced sense of separation between us?

Much of our low-level bickering over the years has been along the lines of: 'You think that's hard? You should try to deal with my challenges . . .' Eventually, I asked myself, what is the truth behind this pattern? Investigating more deeply, I conceded that both of us feel unappreciated by the other, as though we need to spend considerable energy convincing the other of how hard we work, how much we contribute. We both felt resentful that our efforts were never noticed and appreciated, hence, these ridiculous conversations.

To break the circuit, I decided to start expressing more gratitude to Tomek for the work he does to support the family and for the efforts he makes. The Buddha said: 'The greatest gain is to give to others; the greatest loss is to receive without gratitude'. Expressing gratitude feels strange at first—even a little cheesy. Sometimes I hesitated, thinking, *I can't say something like that! It's not me. It's not natural. It's over the top.* These are just thoughts, not truths. Lies, in fact.

Even if we start expressing appreciation in a slightly ironic tone, as I did, it is still powerful and eventually we can move into removing the irony. Once I started expressing appreciation, so did he. When one of those one-upmanship conversations begins, we can try to be mindful of the tug of habit tempting us to plunge in and defend our false sense of a separate self. Then, hopefully, we can label our thoughts 'small mind', and let go.

We are by no means the only couple who experienced a significant breakthrough by learning to express appreciation. My friend Anna, mother of Oscar, wife of Arthur, shared these diary entries:

> Angry, not coping with the day well. I called Arthur to ask him to come home on time. He commented, 'Why do you find everything so hard?'
>
> Sitting in the spare bedroom on strike. Just left Arthur and Oscar to their own devices.
>
> Arthur's comment triggered me. Makes me angry and resentful at all the relentless, boring things I do all day—washing, folding, shopping, putting away shopping, cleaning Oscar's bottom, trying to get him to sleep, making him little meals, cleaning up after him, stacking the dishwasher, unstacking the dishwasher, wiping the bench . . . it's as dull as can be. Then Oscar literally screamed for 40 minutes on waking and was sensitive after that. Seven months pregnant, I'm tired. So I feel deeply undervalued when he asks me why I find it all so hard.

Anna and Arthur managed to turn their situation around with some help from their therapist Gudula, whose advice echoes the Buddha's on gratitude. Anna writes afterwards about the therapy session:

> She explained that when you are employed in paid work you are acknowledged and valued for what you do in many ways. Along with actual money, you have contact with colleagues and feedback from bosses, which all helps create meaningfulness and a sense of recognition for your efforts. Meanwhile, the stay-at-home parents do thankless, invisible work. She told Arthur that he needs to come home and 'see' what I have done. She encouraged him to give me plenty of feedback and acknowledgement as he gets it at work and no one else can give it to me. I need to acknowledge

what he does too both in earning our income and in his role as
dad—that way we'll feel respected and appreciated and not get
competitive over who has the hardest life.

With only occasional lapses, Anna and Arthur have continued to apply
this advice over the years and enjoy the goodwill it creates. I attended
their joint 40th birthday party where they each made moving speeches
full of heartfelt appreciation for each other.

TAKING RESPONSIBILITY

One effective way to turn a relationship around is to ensure that we
have taken full responsibility for our role in any problems. This might
mean taking seriously the content of our partner's criticism, nagging
or more official complaints. Given how easy, and common, it is to
blame our partner for any relationship problems, I find it is worth
pausing occasionally to consider what life might be like living with me.

- **Would I want to be in a relationship with someone like me?**
  The first time I heard a version of this question was when I
  was working for a large company. During a training session the
  facilitator challenged us to ask ourselves: 'Would I want to work
  with someone like me?' I remember feeling a radical shift in
  perspective upon hearing this question. I imagined somebody fresh
  and new joining the company and meeting me (arguably, I used
  to be a tad cynical about many aspects of office life). I started
  paying more attention to the effect of my actions and comments
  around the office. Asking ourselves, 'What's in it for me?' or, 'How
  does that affect me?' has helped humans to survive, but to really
  prosper as a species we might turn this habitual question around

and ask: 'How do I affect you?' We tend to drop our guard with our partners: we are more likely to relax and suspend our usual manners. But does this mean that we rarely smile? That we whine too much? That we forget to be generous, empathic, cheerful?

- **Am I treating my partner the way I would like to be treated?** I often take inspiration from the words of Gandhi, 'Be the change you want to see in the world.' If you want to see your relationship become more loving, considerate, or fun, then *be* more loving, considerate, or fun. Although I usually go to Buddhism for inspiration, when it comes to relationships it's hard to go past the words of Jesus: 'Do unto others . . .'

- **What kind of personal qualities do I aspire to?** Buddhists often use death as a teacher (as we will investigate in Chapter 17) but so did a recent documentary called *Making Couples Happy* in which four struggling couples explored ways to mend their relationships. One exercise required each individual to write their own eulogy, to consider how they would like to be remembered. The process enabled them to identify their values (such as working together as a team, planning their future together, dreaming together, celebrating and remembering good times) and whether they had been living in a way that was true to these values.[6]

- **What would I want for my own children?** Our partner is somebody's precious child. Our partner had parents who ardently wished for the happiness of their child (if they didn't, then they should have). At times when I have felt mean-spirited towards Tomek, I have reminded myself of his mother and how hard she worked for his welfare, how deeply she loved him and how difficult it must have been for her when her only son left Poland. Treating Tomek lovingly is a way of honouring her. I can also borrow her perspective on Tomek: as a mother, she was forgiving, her love unconditional and limitless. When we imagine our own children fully grown and living with partners, we know we want them to be in loving, understanding relationships.

- **What kind of relationship do I model for my children?** The more we can model a loving relationship for them, the better the chances they will live in one themselves. Just as people pay more attention to our body language than our words, our children learn more from our behaviour than our advice.
- **Do I notice the positives?** Do I regularly remind myself of my partner's positive qualities? Do I spend time enjoying them and appreciating them to anywhere like the extent of time I spend thinking about the flaws? Do I express appreciation for those qualities, to my partner, and even to others about my partner?

THINGS TO CONTEMPLATE . . .

- Am I a shit-collector or an egg-collector?
- Can I switch to 'big mind' more often so that I see not just 'my' pain but the universal pain inherent in relationships? Do I need to take it all so personally?
- Do I blame my partner for all our difficulties or have I taken some responsibility?

THINGS TO DO

- Acknowledge your partner's routine efforts in keeping the household running whether it be through paid work, housework or childcare. Express gratitude often.
- Monitor the ratio of positive to negative behaviours towards your partner ensuring they are at least five to one. Water the seeds of joy.

- Make sure you notice and 'take in' any kindnesses from your partner. This means that we:
  —turn positive facts into positive experiences
  —savour the experience
  —relax the body and absorb the experience.
- Don't always trust your memory of your partner's past behaviour. It is reconstructive and prone to bias based on our current mood.
- Be mindful of how you talk about your partner in their absence and any consequences of this. Remember to talk about your partner's positive qualities with others.

being authentic
and present
with our partner

ONE WAY TO MAKE love grow in our relationship is to be more authentic and share more of who we are. Intimacy, to a large extent, comes from revealing vulnerability rather than acting as though we are always strong and problem-free. Sharing about your daily life and feelings is an antidote to the distancing that plagues so many relationships. Kristin Armstrong, ex-wife of disgraced cyclist Lance Armstrong, wrote an article lamenting the way she allowed her authentic self to disappear behind a veneer of dutiful wife and mother. 'The time may come when you realize that the only way to restore the meaning to your marriage is to get back the real you. It requires warrior-size courage to take a stand against the miscommunication, deceptions and emotional distance that breed in the shadows of inauthenticity.'

She ardently hopes that her own young daughters will one day be in relationships where they 'speak from the heart': 'If you have a preference, voice it. If you have a question, ask it. If you want to cry, bawl. If you need help, raise your hand and jump up and down.'[1]

Aware of the vulnerability in another human being, most of us are capable of compassion and empathy and the expression of these qualities helps couples feel closer. When couples feel free to express both good and bad aspects of life, they avoid the dullness that sets in for those who only express the good, or only express the bad.

I felt personally challenged by the words of Kristin Armstrong. In the interests of keeping the peace, in the interests of keeping life simple, had I too lost the 'real me' to any extent? A particular issue between Tomek and I had become too difficult to talk about. Past attempts to resolve it had ended in painful conflict. Had this led to miscommunication, deceptions and emotional distance? To inauthenticity? With the passing of time I had begun to withhold information from Tomek—hiding certain papers, not speaking about some of the major events going on in my mind. I will spare readers the details about our long-running issue—that could take another book to explain—but suffice it to say money was at the centre of it. We tiptoed around our problem, avoiding all mention of it, eventually creating a giant 'elephant in the room'—which we had learnt to live with. It took me a few months to collect up the 'warrior-size courage' but I did it. This time, however, I remembered what had worked most effectively in the past for our relationship and I put all my thoughts into a letter, which I tweaked and perfected until it became a thorough and sensitive expression of my thoughts.

Remembering the Buddha's advice about Skilful Speech being 'at the right time' I waited until a moment when I thought Tomek would be most receptive—about two weeks after writing the letter. I handed it to him before going to collect the boys from a few suburbs away.

'I've written you a letter,' I said.

Tomek groaned and said, 'You've got too much time on your hands.'

I chose to ignore his comment.

The upshot was that after two years of tension around this issue, the letter solved everything. Like magic. Tomek suddenly seemed to understand the situation, and with this, the problem literally disappeared. We barely even needed to speak about the letter and its contents. He wordlessly shifted his point of view and I felt thoroughly understood. I had wasted so many months feeling anxious about this issue, when a simple letter had been the answer all along.

TO SHARE OR NOT TO SHARE?

While intimate sharing can make couples closer, we still need to walk what the Buddha would call, 'the middle road'. No partner should have to become a full-time therapist. Nor should anyone have to put up with a stream of negativity and complaints day after day. Likewise, every partner has the right to some quiet time alone, too.

We don't share our vulnerability with the expectation that our partner will remove our pain. Yet if we can provide each other with acceptance for who we are, flaws and all, then our love can only grow. This is unconditional love and makes each of us feel safe and more likely to open up to the other. This need for acceptance may need spelling out to a partner who feels they must either 'fix' the vulnerabilities they hear about, change the subject or jump out of a moving vehicle. Such reactions suggest an unwillingness to make space for one's own negative emotions—if you can't do it for yourself, it makes it harder to do it for others.

For some of us, sharing vulnerability can seem too threatening. Trust may be the issue for a partner who may have reason to worry about their secrets leaking out to others. I remember feeling horrified at a mother who, over drinks, told all the women assembled about her husband's depression, followed by details from sessions with his psychologist. Alternatively, reluctance to share vulnerabilities may spring from a male need to live up to a gender stereotype of complete self-reliance or emotional invulnerability. Or a partner might have painful memories of times when others ignored, ridiculed or failed to understand disclosures.

Some of us feel ourselves to be not ready to explore vulnerabilities for fear of where this may lead. Yet suppressing what Jungian psychologists call our 'shadow side' can have self-defeating consequences. Our shadow side comes out in ways we are not conscious of, such as when we project the parts of ourselves we cannot own onto others, or our partner, as a way to protect our self-image. I have always been amused to find that those who grumble about the bossiness of others, about how others 'insist on having their own way', tend to be people who I find exceptionally bossy and insistent on their own way. (By the same token, I'm sure there are people who find me bossy and insistent on having my own way.)

With meditation and mindfulness, we become more familiar with our inner world, coming to know our shadow side more fully and taking more responsibility for it. We might also develop a better idea of what we want from a relationship and find the courage to ask for it. We might find that we have been expecting things from our relationship that we should be providing for ourself. Or we might see more clearly what we can let go of any resentments, gripes, or grudges.

HONESTY

In the process of my research, I came across more than one book where the author assumed the voice of an 'expert' addressing the ignorant, a 'holder of all knowledge' obliged to fill the empty vessels. Such experts, for example, usually chose not to disclose any of their own relationship failings.

One book was a glaring exception written by a couple who follow Buddhist teachings. While the authors of *101 Things I Wish I Knew When I Got Married*, couple Linda and Charlie Bloom, were both psychotherapists 'with over fifty-five years of combined experience in relationship counselling', they chose to be refreshingly honest with readers about their shortcomings. As a result, their personalised account of married life felt many times more immediate, compelling, memorable and helpful than other books. I found their willingness to expose the exact things most of us try so hard to hide, even from ourselves, generous in the extreme. Their authenticity provides the perfect model for us to defer to in our own relationships.

Take this impressive example of self-awareness from Charlie Bloom:

To be honest, I am not always perfectly honest . . .
   Lies, no matter how small, always take their toll on the trust,

goodwill, and respect in our relationships. The bad news is that most of us are likely to struggle with issues of deceit throughout our lives. The good news is that as we practice being conscious communicators, we become aware and less tolerant of our own dishonesty . . .

Examples of advantages that I have tried to gain by lying to Linda in the past are: avoiding the possibility of conflict; creating a favorable impression with her; maintaining the upper hand; and wanting to prove that I was good, honourable, superior, intelligent, competent, successful, or some combination of the above. The underlying intention of most of my lies has to do with trying to influence the way Linda perceives me in order to maintain some degree of control in our relationship . . .

Finding the courage and commitment to confront the tendency to lie can add strength, love and integrity to our marriages.[2]

Notably, the first word the Buddha chose to describe Skilful Speech, in the Noble Eightfold Path, was 'truthful'.

IF OUR PARTNER WILL NOT OPEN UP . . .

Our partner may not be the type to discuss emotions, may not experience emotions as deeply as we do, or may not be around much. We do need to respect each other's boundaries. If someone has no desire to share their vulnerabilities at this point in their lives, we let them be. I remember one recently divorced man saying to me: 'My wife always insisted I was an onion and it frustrated her that I wouldn't explore all my layers. But I always felt more like a potato. I was never particularly aware of any layers. I'm just a simple bloke—what you see is what you get!'

Some of us settle for intimate sharing with friends, family members, a therapist, a support group or a diary rather than with our partner. We also have the option of cultivating enviable self-sufficiency and a spiritual practice is helpful on this path. Still, there is no point trying to fool ourselves that we can cope with a life without any warm human connection.

MINDFUL LISTENING

Many a couples therapist teaches the technique known as 'mindful listening'. Each member of the couple has a turn to speak and the listener pays close attention without interrupting or fixing the problem. The therapist typically encourages the couple to use eye contact, empathic nodding and 'aha' sounds. This is effective—of course it is—for many couples who want to feel heard by each other.

Buddhist teacher Gregory Kramer, from the United States, has a far grander vision of how we can practise mindful listening, as part of a practice that can be deeply transformative. With this in mind, Gregory Kramer developed the interpersonal meditation practice known as Insight Dialogue, which he has taught in retreat settings since 1995. It evolved out of Gregory's belief that it is in relationship to others that our reactivity reveals itself, showing us how our various attachments make us suffer.

I attended one of Gregory's week-long retreats where I tasted for myself the fruits of a practice grounded in interpersonal relationships. While some of the meditation sits on Gregory's retreat took place in silence and solitude, in line with the traditional Buddhist retreat, most of the sits involved interacting in pairs. Gregory would set a topic—such as the self, impermanence, or anger—and each pair would engage in a dialogue, at the same time cultivating meditative qualities of the mind, such as mindfulness and concentration. Participants learnt that there is more to mindful communication than mere 'paying attention'. While on day one, we focused on only the first of the six instructions, with each passing day Gregory added further instructions for us to practise in pairs. We engaged in our dialogues with a series of partners and Gregory would ring a bell once or twice throughout each sit to remind us of the latest instruction:

1. **Pause**

   Practising 'Pause' is a way to intercept the habit-driven flow of an interaction and return to the present. During a pause, we might tune into bodily sensations, inner reactions, or tensions. In surrendering to the pause we effectively 'let go' of the power of our automatic tendencies.

2. **Relax**

   To relax is simply to release any bodily tension found when we pause. We also 'relax' the mind and we do this by bringing an attitude of acceptance to the moment, towards our partner, our self, our thoughts or any of the details of the situation. To relax is to choose ease over tension.

3. **Open**

   To open is to extend our awareness to our partner and to the setting. We open to images, sounds and what our partner is telling us. The sense of separation may decrease as what is routinely an experience of 'self and other' becomes, rather, awareness of experience.

4. **Trust emergence**

   Recognising impermanence, the inevitability of change, we drop any agenda or desire to control the conversation: any desire to impress, to reinforce a self-image, to control what happens next. Rather, we dwell in goal-free insecurity and unpredictability.

5. **Listen deeply**

   We pay attention to what our partner says. Curious in attitude, we silently ask the question, 'What is happening now?' Listening kindly to a fellow human being, we allow their words to call forth compassion within us. We listen to the words and the way their meaning unfolds in our mind. We notice the emotional tone, the body language and our own reactions.

6. **Speak the truth**

   This does not mean we say what may be inappropriate, private, or harmful. We practise the Buddha's right speech from the Eightfold Path (speech that is true, timely, kind, useful and well-intentioned). Of course, by 'the truth' Gregory only means the subjective truth of our own experience and we can only know this truth if we are mindful to our inner experience. This is the most difficult instruction for applying mindfulness: speaking tends to challenge our capacity to be present. Mindful speaking takes practice.

As Gregory says, practising mindfulness in solitude does help to bring mindfulness into our interactions with others. Being mindful while engaging in a dialogue, however, is a way to integrate the benefits of an established meditation practice into our entire lives. With so much of our suffering due to relationship difficulties, it makes sense to treat our conversations with others as rich ground for practice.

THINGS TO CONTEMPLATE . . .

- Is our relationship a safe space for intimate sharing or are there problems with trust, or being taken seriously?
- Do I accuse others of the flaws I cannot own in myself?

- Can I respect my partner's boundaries if my partner chooses to keep parts of themself private?

THINGS TO DO

- Aim for an authentic relationship where both of you feel free to open up and talk about what is important to you.
- Practise mindful listening with Gregory Kramer's six components: pause, relax, open, trust emergence, listen deeply, speak the truth.

CHAPTER 16

cultivating love

A FEW YEARS AGO I attended a week-long 'Dharma gathering' full of workshops and discussion groups about applying Buddhist teachings to our lives. In one of the workshops the Buddhist teacher split us into groups, armed with butcher's paper and textas, and instructed us to brainstorm answers to the question, 'How can I be more loving?'

I was not impressed.

I attended the gathering to learn more about challenging Buddhist scriptures and stimulating Buddhist concepts. I was not here to sit around with a bunch of hippies talking about 'lurve'. I shared my attitude problem with my friend after the workshop but she only said, 'It's a very good question though, don't you think?' I couldn't see it at the time. I was too blocked, too cool and superior. In retrospect, however, I wonder why I was so hard-edged. Western Buddhists in my Theravadin tradition tend to intellectualise their practice and resist anything that feels lowbrow so I guess I was conforming to stereotype. Years down the track, however, I wonder if that question *How can I be more loving?* might be the most important we ever ask. As senior Buddhist teacher Jack Kornfield wrote, 'At the end of life, our questions are very simple: did I live fully? Did I love well?'[1]

I decided to canvass some contacts from my Buddhist community in search of creative answers to this question. My Buddhist friend Anna shared this:

Arthur and I are both big list writers and annotators of our marriage. So we have a *Book of Marriage* with all sorts of slightly embarrassing things in it. Each year on our anniversary we go out to a nice restaurant and do a review of the year. Flipping back through these, the headings we've come up with include: our five highlights, five lowlights, favourite things about Anna/Arthur, what I'd like changed in Anna/Arthur, what I have appreciated about Anna/Arthur, one thing that drives me nutty, ten things I love about parenting Oscar and Sam.

Also, after hard times we often write it all out. One page of the book is entitled 'The Time of Great Misgivings'. It outlines what just went wrong and what we could do about it. We did this, for example, after Arthur's retrenchment experience a few years ago.

Anna has also invented a name for a simple gesture I have heard numerous women rave about:

Cotib stands for cup of tea in bed. I'm trying to introduce the word cotib into the dictionary as my legacy! Cotibs are a highlight of my married life. There is no better way to wake up than to have Arthur present me with a steaming hot cup of tea, and then read in bed or do a Sudoku. I can't express how much I love it. It is a beautiful gift from Arthur that makes me really appreciate being married. My grandfather always brought my grandmother a cotib every morning. So I see it as following a family tradition.

One friend of mine came close to having an affair and chose to discuss her confused feelings with her husband—who felt devastated. When she finally decided to forgo the affair and re-commit to her partner, they went through a beautiful period of reconnecting to each other. At the time she told me that every night, before they went to bed, they would read a page or two from a tiny book by Stephanie Dowrick, *The Almost-Perfect Marriage*, a collection of inspiring quotations. They would read a page and reflect on how it applied to their marriage. A sample page from the book:

Empathy is vital to intimacy.

Empathy doesn't mean feeling the emotions someone else is experiencing.

It means understanding and validating those feelings. 'I am not in your shoes, but I do care about what you are experiencing.'[2]

Here is another:

There is always more than one way to interpret a situation.
No one needs to be wrong.

Another activity that automatically deepens the connection is to meditate together as a couple. Robin, the psychotherapist and couples counsellor from my meditation group, has been doing this with her husband for an impressive 35 years. She talks about the benefits.

A daily meditation sit has been a wonderful practice and common passion I have shared with my husband since we met. At that time I believed that since life's greatest joys and sorrows arose in relationships, it seemed natural that a shared daily mindfulness practice should be key to our future happiness, and it continues to be. Our practice together creates a precious space where we can *be*, belong and become.

If a shared meditation sit is raising the bar way too high, we can try something simpler, like a mindful hug. Thich Nhat Hanh runs a retreat centre in France called Plum Village. Over the years he found Westerners wanted to give him a hug of appreciation, and since this was not familiar behaviour for a Vietnamese, let alone a monk, he felt awkward.

I decided that if I wanted to work with friends in the West, I would have to learn the culture of the West, so I invented hugging meditation . . . According to the practice, you have to really hug the person you are hugging. You have to make him or her very real in your arms . . . breathing consciously and hugging with all your body, spirit, and heart. Hugging meditation is a practice of mindfulness. 'Breathing in, I know my dear one is in my arms, alive. Breathing out, she is so precious to me.' If you breathe deeply like that, holding the person you love, the energy of care, love, and mindfulness will penetrate into that person and she will be nourished and bloom like a flower.[3]

With all due respect to Thich Nhat Hanh, I suspect he might not have been the first to invent hugging meditation. Maybe the first to name it. As something I strive to engage in regularly with Tomek, I do recommend it.

Along with *How can I be more loving?* many of us may need to ask, *What should I suggest to my partner to do to help me feel more loved?* After all, many of us silently fume about partners who love us but don't express their love in a way we appreciate. They might fail to speak what couples therapists call our 'love language'. While one partner expresses love through practical chores, another expects verbal expression or physical affection. Rather than wait many decades for our partner to read our mind, we can always tell them what makes us feel cared for.

. . . AND SMILE, SMILE, SMILE

One way to be more loving towards our partner is to smile. Now, I realise that this might sound a little elementary, even a bit Sunday

school (if you're happy and you know it . . .) but some of us are slow
learners. Let me give an example.

In my late twenties I resigned from a job as a corporate trainer
and had to attend an 'exit interview' with Andrew from the human
resources department. One of his questions generated a memorable
conversation for me.

'Who would you say are the two people you most admire in this
company?' Andrew asked.

'Probably Elaine upstairs and maybe . . . um . . . you,' I replied.

'Really?' responded Andrew, looking confused. 'I always got the
sense you never liked me much.'

Now it was my turn to be surprised. I loved Andrew. Everyone
did. He was hilarious, mischievous, fun. How could he think I didn't
like him? I asked him to explain but he was non-committal. 'Dunno.
Just got that impression.'

A few years later I had a similar conversation with someone else
who confronted me for not liking them even though I definitely did.
I remembered my conversation with Andrew, along with all those
random middle-aged men over the years, in shops and other public
places, who had felt the need to say to me: 'Cheer up love, it can't
be all that bad.'

Eventually the unfortunate truth dawned on me. My face, at
rest, does not exude friendliness. It's fine if I smile—I'm a ravishing
beauty of wide renown when I smile—but often I forget to. These
days, it is more important than ever for me to smile during social
interactions. Approaching the age of 47 my face, at rest is not looking
much friendlier. In fact, it manages to look angry and sad and even
tired, all at the same time. Some say that by middle age we have the
face we deserve. I reject that.

Why am I telling you this? It is a sad fact of life that as we grow
older, frown marks deepen, mouths turn down, eyes become hooded

and we generally look grumpier. From looking at our partner's face, many of us will assume our partner is angry with us, sulking or displeased. This may not, necessarily, be the case. We can, of course, check whether this phenomenon is occurring in our relationship by sneaking a peak at our partner's face as they watch television. Are they looking more grumpy with the passage of time? If so, we can learn to take facial expressions less at face value (so to speak).

Some of us, such as myself, will need to smile at our partner more often as we age in order to avoid appearing glum. This is no great sacrifice though, as smiling tends to make the smiler feel better. The smile-ee also benefits: if Tomek walks into the living room after work with a smile on his face I instantly relax and feel open to his presence. Given my own grumpy face, I try to smile at Tomek as often as possible. He often smiles back.

Another reason to reflect on our smiling habits is that the smile is a component of our body language. While most of us assume the words we say are the most powerful component of our message, the opposite is true. If someone perceives a mismatch between our words and our body language, then they are far more likely to rely on our body language. Body language speaks louder than words.

By our thirties and forties, most of us realise the importance of facial expressions and remember to smile frequently during social interactions. With our partner, in our own homes, however, we are more inclined to drop such niceties. Yet a smile takes so little effort and makes such a difference to the emotional climate. It is an act of generosity, or consideration, for others.

Granted, fake smiles—which might even look like grimaces or leers—can be off-putting and some people have less convincing fake smiles than others. The remedy, in such cases, is to remove any fakery by ensuring our smile is genuine. This takes mindfulness: we consciously enjoy the act of smiling by focusing on the physical sensations, the release of tension, the intention to be loving, or the appreciation of our partner that comes with smiling.

A smiler feels better too. In a favourite study of mine, one group of participants held a pen in their mouth horizontally, with their teeth, thus creating, in effect, a fake smile, while in another group participants held the pen with their lips, creating a pout. Both groups, unaware of the aim of the experiment, then watched cartoons. The group with the enforced smiles reported finding the cartoons significantly more amusing than the group whose smiles were disabled.[4] The study supports the idea that our facial expression has an effect on how we feel and that even fake smiles might do us more good than their reputation suggests.

CULTIVATE SHARED FRIENDSHIPS

The *Mangala Sutta* is a stretch of Buddhist scripture where the Buddha listed the greatest blessings for which we should both strive and feel grateful. He listed items such as residing in a suitable locality, a peaceful occupation and the cherishing of family members. Very first on the list, however, was 'associating with the wise'. The Buddha encouraged us to associate with those who have the qualities we seek to cultivate in ourselves. 'If one wants to be patient, be around those who are patient . . . If one wants to be generous, be around those who are generous.' So the Buddha encourages us to choose friends who inspire us, who are in tune with our values and who bring out the best in us.

An interesting question for people in relationships is to what extent our friends, those who can potentially inspire us, are shared. This became a focus for me after I came across some very stark results of a study of over 2000 respondents conducted over twenty years in the United States. The conclusions suggested that couples with no shared friendships had way more marital problems than those who shared all their friends. Couples with *some* shared friends did have fewer problems than the 'no friends shared group' but did not enjoy the same protection from problems as the 'all friends shared' group. The reasons for such a finding remain unknown.[5]

Yikes, I thought. Tomek and I have some shared friends but they all live outside Sydney so we rarely see them. Otherwise, our closest friends are all relatively unshared. I never meet his car-racing friends or work colleagues. He rarely meets my closest friends, who I mainly catch up with on girls' nights or when Tomek is at work. It's all a bit like Saudi Arabia. This disturbs me but ultimately it is just another unresolvable imperfection of our relationship to add to the list and try to accept.

So while it would be ideal for couples to associate with shared friends who all inspire each other, this may or may not be happening for us. It is certainly something to appreciate if it is, seek out if it's not, or accept if it won't.

LOVINGKINDNESS MEDITATION

To consciously wish our partner well as part of a meditation, or at quiet moments throughout our day, is a way to enhance our connection.

The traditional lovingkindness meditation involves phrases such as, *May she be happy, May he be free from suffering, May I be safe*. We start by saying these phrases about ourselves, then someone we love, then a neutral person in our lives, a difficult person, and finally all beings everywhere. The idea is to cultivate feelings, not so much thoughts, of lovingkindness. While some Buddhists adore this practice, particularly the Tibetans, in my experience most don't.

Complaints I've heard include: 'It's too forced', 'It doesn't feel natural for me', 'Sending lovingkindness to the difficult person feels fake or like a denial of what I really feel.' Many Buddhist teachers feel the same too. Yet some of these teachers still urge us to stay open to the power of this meditation. For starters, just observing our own aversion to it can be revealing. Why is it so hard to feel loving? What are the obstacles? The blockages?

Many teachers encourage us to fiddle with the phrases and come up with ones that feel more original and meaningful: *May I feel comforted, May he feel cared for, May she feel cradled in the arms of lovingkindness.* One hinting at the value of acceptance goes: *May I feel happy just as I am in my current circumstances.*

Other teachers suggest we drop the phrases altogether and cultivate the feeling: using images, or memories of moments when we felt lovingkindness spontaneously arise. They teach that the purpose is to immerse ourselves in the feeling, to really pause and take it in.

The Buddha, in the *Metta Sutta,* put it like this:

Avoiding any mean deeds blameworthy by the wise.
Thinking always thus: 'May all beings be happy and safe,
May they all have tranquil minds.'
Whatsoever pulsates with the breath of life . . .
May they all be happy.
May no-one deceive another, nor despise him in anyway
    anywhere.
Let no-one wish another ill, owing to anger or provocation.
Just as a mother would protect her child—her only child—
    with her life—even so let us cultivate this boundless love to
    all living beings.
Radiating with a full heart loving thoughts of kindness towards
    all the world,

Free from anger, malice or anxiety—above, below and in all
   directions.

The Buddha challenges us to see our partners from the perspective of
a mother. This does not mean picking up their socks or reminding
them where they have to be, but rather in treasuring, in recognising
the preciousness of another human being.

Subhana Barzaghi, a senior Buddhist teacher in both the Zen and
Theravadin traditions, is one of the teachers that chooses to emphasise
love. She draws on the Buddhist simile that describes practice as a bird
with two wings: one wing is wisdom, one is love. Without both the
bird will not fly. An avid collector of quotations about love, Subhana
offers these from Indian teacher Nisargadatta Maharaj:

Wisdom tells me I am nothing. Love tells me I am everything.
Between the two my life flows.

And:

Mind creates the abyss, the heart crosses it.

Should you go on a retreat led by Subhana, you discover her passion
for the Sufi poets, particularly Hafiz. Given half a chance, Subhana
loves nothing more than to read poems such as this one, 'With That
Moon Language' by Hafiz:

Admit something:
Everyone you see, you say to them, 'Love me.'
Of course you do not do this out loud, otherwise someone
   would call the cops.
Still, though, think about this, this great pull in us to connect.

Why not become the one who lives with a full moon in each eye
That is always saying,
With that sweet moon language,
What every other eye in this world is dying to hear?

THINGS TO CONTEMPLATE . . .

- Am I cynical about love or expressions of love? Does it feel too
  cheesy, schmaltzy, corny for me? If so, is there a cost to my
  relationship in this attitude? Does it mean I never say, or enact,
  the things my partner most wants from me? The things that could
  make us feel close?

THINGS TO DO

- Challenge yourself at every opportunity: how can I be more loving?
- Consider: list-keeping, cotib, reading an inspirational book
  together, shared meditation sits, hugging meditation.
- Smile as an act of generosity for your partner.
- Ensure your smile is not fake by cultivating the feelings that go
  behind a genuine smile.
- Seek out and treasure shared friendships with people who inspire
  you both or share your values. Practise acceptance if this is too hard.
- Wish your partner well during meditation or at any point
  throughout your day: *May she be happy, May he be well, May he
  feel loved, May she feel safe.*

CHAPTER 17

sorting out what really matters

WHEN IT COMES TO tools for reflection, nothing beats death—in Buddhism, death is acknowledged as a valuable teacher. In some countries, Buddhists meditate in cemeteries; in others, they meditate on the process of decay of the human body. While Westerners will not be in a hurry to follow suit, we can still learn from death if we are prepared to stop living in denial of its inevitability.

My first glimpse of death as a teacher was probably not a typical one. When I was in my twenties I worked with a memorable woman called Sandra, who used to work at a funeral parlour. She told me her story. One day, a wealthy man in a suit dropped in to make arrangements for the funeral of his recently deceased wife. As Sandra dealt with him, he answered several calls on his mobile phone relating to urgent business deals. At the end of their meeting, Sandra watched him jump into his convertible and drive away and she thought to herself, 'He seems so untouched by his wife's death. With his brisk, business-like manner, he could have been organising the sale of a house.'

Then she froze. It suddenly occurred to her, 'That's exactly how my own husband would behave if it was me in that coffin.' With that realisation, she began arrangements to divorce him. She never regretted her decision and is now happily remarried.

When the Buddha, or Prince Siddhartha as he was originally named, was growing up, his father went to great lengths to protect him from any knowledge of the suffering in the world outside the palace walls. When Siddhartha finally sneaked outside to take a look he was struck, and deeply disturbed, by the pain involved in birth, sickness, aging and death and this propelled his spiritual seeking. In the Western world, we live in a society that, like the Buddha's father, tries to ignore the painful, troubling aspects of life. Given that death is the only certainty, the only event we can count on, Buddhists strive to acknowledge it.

For couples, the certainty of death, and the uncertainty around exactly when it will occur, can affect our lives together. I thought I would explore exactly how, with the help of an oncologist.

INTERVIEW WITH AN ONCOLOGIST

I am fortunate to have one excellent contact to ask what death can teach us about relationships. Jonathan Page has been the chairman of my Buddhist group for several years and has some decades of experience as an oncologist treating cancer patients. Referring to his compassion, I've heard more than a few fellow meditators say, 'If you ever got cancer, you'd want Jonathan as your doctor.' He has spent many hours sitting beside his patients as life has slipped away from them. He has also completed a course run by Buddhist teacher Subhana, entitled 'If I had only a year to live', which encourages reflection on how to use our lives meaningfully.

Jonathan is highly dedicated to his Buddhist practice, even teaching introductory courses in Buddhism, as well as meditation courses for fellow doctors. Years ago he said to me, 'I don't look back on my day and judge it for how much I got done. I look back and ask, "How present was I?"' I have often reminded myself of those words and aspire to reach that stage myself.

Jonathan agreed to meet me for coffee one afternoon to talk about death. I started by asking Jonathan, 'You've been in the position of working with numerous couples to help them through the journey that follows a cancer diagnosis. What kind of effect does a diagnosis have on a couple?'

'It depends on the couple,' Jonathan answered. 'I especially enjoy dealing with some of the older couples who have been together for decades and are infinitely accommodating of their sick partner and all their needs. To use the words of one old gentleman, "What do you expect? I've been married to the woman I love for sixty years!"'

Jonathan smiles at the recollection, adding, 'Another elderly man always refers to his wife as "the bride".'

'How about the younger couples?' I asked.

'Some are very close and supportive. Some break up,' Jonathan answered.

'Are you telling me that some people just up and leave as soon as the going gets too tough?' I asked, appalled.

'Well, the emotions around cancer can be very extreme, and for some people, unmanageable. They find it too scary. They need to disappear.'

I was impressed that Jonathan managed to sound so non-judgemental. 'I guess it's just immaturity, on their part,' I offered, in an attempt to sound less harsh.

'How about the more inspiring partners?' I asked. 'How do they respond to life after a diagnosis?'

'Sometimes I get to see unconditional love. That's a love that transcends physical appearance, strong emotions and change. Unconditional love doesn't rely on a partner having a fixed identity. It's more flexible and accommodating to the unpredictability of life.'

'So what are the signs, that you notice, of this unconditional love?' I inquired.

'I guess one strong indicator is when partners talk about "our cancer", or "our chemo",' Jonathan answered.

'Kind of like when couples talk about "our" pregnancy,' I suggested, remembering when Tomek declared, 'I'm never going through pregnancy again!'

'So, for the loving couples,' I continued, 'how might a cancer diagnosis change their approach to life?'

'Well, say a couple successfully complete chemotherapy and are given a good prognosis. Many such couples reappraise their lives. Some find themselves with a whole new project where they seek answers to questions like: "Where do we find meaning?" "What in our lives is not so meaningful, that we could afford to give up or let go?" They see life through clearer eyes. They have a feeling for their own mortality and a sense of what they want do with their time.'

'So what sort of changes might they make?'

'Some patients decide they want to spend more time with their children. Others, the opposite! They might recognise they had a suffocating relationship with their children and they loosen their attachment, or free their children from all the demands and expectations they inflicted on them. Sometimes they can start to see their partner, too, as a person in their own right, a more independent person, rather than with attachment. It's not unheard of that patients can be grateful for their cancer, for the way it changes their perceptions.'

'So can cancer open up a spiritual side in patients and their partners?' I asked.

'It can certainly be a beautiful entry into the nature of perception. For many it's an opportunity to move to a new level, a bigger picture of life that's more clear and luminous. They start to perceive the wonder and preciousness of life and relationships.'

'I guess in some cases that can happen for the patient but not their partner?'

'Yes. Sometimes, normal life takes on a kind of unreality for the patient. The mindless dream they were living shatters. Everybody around them is living on automatic pilot, or in what some Buddhists might call a dream state—or just unawake. The cancer crisis might pass and everybody else returns back to the fantasy. They're back in the movie, and the patient is left wishing their partner too, or other loved ones, could have shifted out of that.'

'How many of your patients, would you say, experience the kind of shift you're describing?'

'I'd say about half. And predominantly older patients. They seem to be more accepting and open to learning. Many choose not to deal, psychologically, with what they have been through. It's interesting, some entertain two conflicting views at the same time: it happened, it didn't happen. A kind of shock and disbelief: did that really happen? They're not in the habit of testing their own perceptions, sorting out what is real and what is not.'

'So if that's the experience of people who survive their diagnosis, how about others who you need to tell something like, "You have a 30 per cent chance of the cancer returning?"'

'In a way this is a gift too. There might be no such thing as returning to "normal life" again. There is no safety, no solid ground. We spend our lives striving for a false sense of security and predictability but it's actually a more realistic way to live when we acknowledge the certainty of death and that we don't know when it will happen. This can change the way we approach each moment: time is precious and we concentrate on what matters, letting the less important fall away. We spend more time in reflection and questioning too.'

'From what you can gather, does cancer change a couple's relationships outside the partnership?'

'It's true that people discover who their friends are. Often there is a culling of friends. Some friends who were once close don't know what to say and end up avoiding their friend with cancer. Or friends once considered not so close turn out to be the most committed.'

At the risk of veering off the subject of couples I could not resist asking, 'What do you think people should say to someone with cancer?'

'"It must be so hard for you," is often all you need to say, although often this is guaranteed to make the person cry. Or you could say, "I can imagine you must be struggling". I do find older people with some life experience are better at this. Recently a 30-year-old man, both a patient and a friend, died of cancer. At his funeral, there was lots of crying and sadness yet through all the time I spent at his bedside, I had never seen any of these people visit him. It's such a missed opportunity for them to use their time meaningfully.'

Reluctant to pass a final judgement, however, Jonathan adds: 'Then again, maybe they did visit when I wasn't around and I guess I don't know what was in their minds during the long illness. Maybe fear. Or they may have felt a visit to be an intrusion.'

'You must also see partners dealing with loss and bereavement.'

'The saving grace of bereavement is that you are only in pain because of the depth of your love. Love can balance out the sadness.'

When we do find ourselves grieving the loss of a loved one, the most important things to do from a Buddhist perspective are to be kind to ourselves and allow ourselves the space to grieve. We don't need to listen to those who believe we 'should have got over it by now' nor those who, with the best of intentions, expect us to cheer up and return to normal. Neither should we use Buddhist teachings to talk ourselves out of our bad feelings: *Death is unavoidable! Everybody dies. Where's your equanimity? Too much attachment!* Rather, we accept that we feel sad, that sadness is a natural part of life, and we practise unconditional self-compassion.

ARE THE TEACHINGS MAKING A DIFFERENCE?

While death is an excellent tool for reflection, so are direct questions such as, *Is Buddhism really making any difference to my life?* The

Buddha didn't expect us to take any of his teachings on faith. He challenged us to try them out for ourselves to see if they work. To quote the Buddha:

> Try something that I have discovered, and then judge it for yourself. If it is good for you, accept it. Otherwise, don't accept it.

This suggests that we need to reflect on the teachings and how they work in our lives and ask ourselves, *Are they really making any difference to my life, to how I relate to others, to how I respond to my circumstances?*

I decided to put this question to Robin, the psychotherapist and couples counsellor from my Buddhist group. Knowing she has a practice spanning four decades, I asked her to write me a paragraph or two on how her mindfulness practice and her daily meditation, which she does together with her husband, affects her life and relationships.

> A daily practice of mindfulness is the antidote to living my life unconsciously and becoming lost in the mind's natural propensity to find fault. It transforms the suffering and conflict that arises into increased insight, loving understanding, compassion and equanimity.
>
> At the same time, the Noble Eightfold Path, with its emphasis on skilful speech, makes me vitally aware of my need to be mindful in conversation as well as on the cushion and to be assertive if that is what I feel is needed.
>
> Buddhist practice helps me remember what I am grateful for in our life together, what is important at the end of our life, and our commitment to make life wonderful regardless of life's inevitable suffering.

USING THE NOBLE EIGHTFOLD PATH AS A TOOL FOR REFLECTION

Not long after I met Tina at my Buddhist group, she moved with her partner to a country town, seeking a lifestyle that aligned with their values. She is a family counsellor and her partner works in environmental education. Committed to her practice, she explains here how she uses the Buddha's Eightfold Path to reflect on her relationship:

The Four Noble Truths have helped me to realise that there is *dukkha*, or suffering, in relationships, and the 'always happy' relationship I had been hunting for is not possible. Then having a way out of *dukkha* with the Eightfold Path has given me hope and a vision for how I can work on our marriage (or work on myself).

I think about the Path when it seems like our marriage is veering off the rails. Working with the first component of the path, **Skilful View**, means working with my vision of the relationship. As it is overall a supportive relationship, my vision is to get over any 'bump' so we can get back to more of a focus of lovingkindness, rather than 'leave when the going gets tough'.

Skilful Thought is about having the right attitude. It helps to remind myself that if I am angry with my partner, we need to address the issue, but I still want to keep the attitude that this marriage and friendship is more important than holding onto anger.

Skilful Speech, is like my north star, to help keep me on track. Even when I am overwhelmed with frustration at my partner, I try to be mindful about my communication and mindful too that **skilful action** follows on from skilful speech or our communication would be meaningless. For me skilful speech includes drawing on my training in nonviolent communication methods, focusing on any unmet needs—mine and his—and avoiding the language of blame.

Another area where **Skilful Action** is a useful focus is in how we sustain ourselves. We both think it's important to grow organic food and tread lightly on the earth. Growing our own fruits and vegetables helps bond us together in what we think is Skilful Action.

I was attracted to my partner because, like me, he values a focus on **Skilful Livelihood**. We both work in areas that although not well paid, give us satisfaction through our belief that we contribute positively to the world. This is a bond we share, which reminds us of our priorities.

Skilful Effort, or putting some work into a relationship, is essential for any marriage but I find the ratio is important too. Sometimes, if I'm putting a huge amount of effort into the marriage, and it's not reciprocated, I can feel resentful. If I talk to my partner about it and pull back on my effort, he will mostly step in to try to even up the 'Skilful Effort' scale. Effort helps to build up the reserves of 'goodwill' in the relationship, that we may need at times of stress.

To be able to see some of the stressful patterns emerging in our relationship I rely on **Skilful Mindfulness**. Having time to garden and meditate each day creates the space for awareness to arise about all areas of my relationship.

Lastly, **Skilful Concentration** helps in many areas including the bedroom, where I find focused concentration is useful for the sexual connection—and also for getting to sleep. If I'm tossing and turning it's often because thoughts are racing around my head. If I meditate on my breathing, I can calm myself down enough to fall asleep. Then all of us are more rested, and happier, in the morning.

Since all the Buddha's teachings fall under one of the components of the Eightfold Path, it makes a handy checklist when we are trying to work out what might need some attention in our relationship, or any other aspect of our lives.

THINGS TO CONTEMPLATE . . .

- What difference has my knowledge of Buddhist teachings made to my life, and my relationship with my partner, so far?

THINGS TO DO

- Remind yourself, from time to time, that death is the only certainty. Let this knowledge be your teacher, especially when it comes to clarifying priorities.
- Follow Tina's example and consider your relationship in the light of the Buddha's Noble Eightfold Path.

some concluding points

IT WOULD BE DISINGENUOUS of me to reach this point in the book without addressing what, for some readers, may be the elephant in the room. I can hear them shouting at me: 'BUT SIDDHARTHA GAUTAMA LEFT HIS WIFE AND BABY!' And not before they named their baby Rahula, which means, curiously, fetter or shackle. Reading this book is effectively taking relationship advice from a man who appears to have abandoned his marriage in a quest to end suffering.

How can we reconcile this inconvenient truth? To a modern-day Westerner many of the traditional 'excuses' are not adequate:

- The Buddha was a prince from a privileged family, so it was not as though his wife Yasodhara and baby Rahula would be left destitute.
- When he left, he seems to have been what we would call today 'depressed'. After years hidden in a palace he felt disillusioned after finally escaping his father's watchful eyes and seeing real life: the suffering inherent in birth, sickness, aging and death.

- To renounce material comfort and wander in search of spiritual enlightenment was a relatively common lifestyle choice in the Buddha's time.
- It is hard to imagine that the words 'co-parenting', or even 'parenting', existed in the Buddha's time.
- We could argue that the positive effect of the Buddha on the lives of millions of people over time—and the fact that he remains a major influence over 2500 years later—justifies his actions.

It did all seem to work out for Yasodhara and her son, who both eventually became followers of the Buddha. This suggests there were no hard feelings, at least in the long run. Both mother and son also achieved enlightenment. They definitely came out ahead.

Still, the best explanation I have heard for Siddhartha abandoning his family is a very simple one. He was not enlightened at the time. If he had been, he would doubtless have stuck around.

•

Lazing on the back porch one Sunday afternoon with Tomek, I broached a topic.

'I've noticed,' I began tentatively, 'that for a few months now you've seemed really happy. Happier than I've seen you for a long time. Is there any particular reason, do you think?'

'No, not really,' Tomek answered.

'Oh, come on,' I urged gently. 'I've really noticed a difference and it would really help me as an author and as a wife to know if there was something in particular.'

'I guess I've just tried to be more conscious of my behaviour,' Tomek answered.

'Wow!' I enthused. 'That's so Buddhist! What do you mean by that exactly? Was there a triggering event? Was it a sudden realisation or a gradual realisation—'

Tomek groaned. 'You ask so many questions. Let's just leave it at that.'

So I did.

I have never reached the stage of my friend Beth who daily held hands with her husband and traded appreciative statements and I don't think I ever will, but that doesn't seem to matter anymore. I feel sure that just expressing appreciation more often has been a major component of the improvements we have enjoyed. How could we have overlooked something so simple, something quite easy to do? It's not expensive. It's not time-consuming. And the act of expressing makes us feel good too. It does take the ability to let go. We've both had some letting go to do—of past hurts, of lingering resentments, of our need to win an argument—and Tomek is probably more gifted at this than me.

acknowledgements

ALTHOUGH HE WILL PROBABLY never read these words, I do acknowledge and thank Tomek. I am fortunate to have a husband whose self-esteem is so intact that he is relatively unconcerned over what I write about him. If it was me, or most other people, we would be checking up on every word to guard our public image (psychologists call this 'impression management'). Tomek is strong enough to not rely on the approval of others and without this unique quality in him I would not have enjoyed the freedom to disclose so many vignettes from our daily life.

Buddhist teachers I am indebted to include Subhana Barzaghi, Geoff Dawson, Victor von der Heyde, Jason Siff, Stephen Batchelor, Jack Kornfield, Winton Higgins, Chris MacLean, Joyce Kornblatt and Gregory Kramer.

Thanks to Dr Jonathan Page who, despite his important work with cancer patients, generously gave me some quality time.

Writers I am grateful to for their time and generous permission include Kristin Neff, author of *Self-Compassion*, Joshua Coleman, author of *The Lazy Husband*, Bettina Arndt, author of *The Sex Diaries*,

Linda and Charlie Bloom authors of *101 Things I Wish I Knew About Marriage,* Rick Hanson author of *Buddha's Brain,* and Lori Brotto for her work on mindfulness and its application in sexual relationships.

Julie Fitness, professor at Macquarie University, helped me to locate many of the studies quoted throughout this book and, without even knowing it, planted many of the seeds that led me to write it.

My dear friend Anna, with the support of her husband Arthur, generously provided many stories from her own relationship and loads of enthusiasm and support for the project as a whole.

Thank you to my spiritual friends who patiently and generously exchanged numerous emails with me about their relationships. I felt truly supported in my work by your willingness to contribute. Particularly Robin Evans but also Tina, Hamish and Nina Drummond, Andrea, Jenny, Danielle, Beth, 'Moira', Joanne, Carlos and Viv.

I also thank Tony Trimingham and Sandra Lines, my excellent trainers and mentors from Family Drug Support.

Much gratitude also to Annette Barlow and Angela Handley at Allen & Unwin, editor Aziza Kuypers, my Mum, Dad, Amanda, Jane, Zac and Alex.

notes

Introduction

1. K. Maezen Miller, *Momma Zen: Walking the crooked path of motherhood*, Trumpeter: Boston, 2006, p. 147.

Chapter 1—The difficulty of living as a couple

1. Wikipedia, 'Divorce Demography', 2013. <http://en.wikipedia.org/wiki/Divorce_demography> (10 August 2013).
2. T.N. Bradbury, F.D. Fincham and S.R. Beach, 'Research on the nature and determinants of marital satisfaction: A decade in review', *Journal of Marriage and the Family*, 2000, vol. 62, pp. 964–80.
3. M.D. Bramlett, and W.D. Mosher, 'First Marriage Dissolution, Divorce, and Remarriage: United States', *Division of Vital Statistics*, 2001, vol. 323, p. 9.
4. D. Sollee, 'What's your relationship IQ?', *Smart Marriages*, 2007. <www.smartmarriages.com/relationship.IQ.html> (10 August 2013).
5. C.R. Knee, 'Implicit theories of relationships: Assessment and prediction of romantic relationship initiation, coping, and longevity', *Journal of Personality and Social Psychology*, 1998, vol. 74, pp. 360–70.
6. His Holiness the Dalai Lama and H.C. Cutler, *The Art of Happiness: A handbook for living*, Hodder: Sydney, 2005, p. 104.
7. R.J. Sternberg, 'Triangulating love', in R.J. Sternberg and M.L. Barnes (eds), *The Psychology of Love*, New Haven, CT: Yale University Press, 1988, pp. 408, 424.

8.   L. Bennetts, 'Science tries analysing love', *The New York Times*, 1978. <http://news.google.com/newspapers?nid=1665&dat=19780731&id=MG4dAAAAIBAJ&sjid=TCQEAAAAIBAJ&pg=6864,3212420> (10 August 2013).

9.   L.J. Waite, D. Browning, W.J. Doherty, M. Gallagher, Y. Luo and S.M. Stanley, *Does Divorce Make People Happy? Findings from a study of unhappy marriages*, Institute of American Values: New York, 2002, pp. 1–39.

10. O.A. Becker and D. Lois, 'Selection, alignment, and their interplay: Origins of lifestyle homogamy in couple relationships', *Journal of Marriage and Family*, 2010, vol. 72, pp. 1234–48.

Chapter 2—Letting go

1.   E. Gilbert, *Committed: A sceptic makes peace with marriage*, Bloomsbury: London, 2010, p. 43.

2.   U. Gupta and P. Singh, 'Exploratory study of love and liking and type of marriages', *Indian Journal of Applied Psychology*, 1982, vol. 19, pp. 699–724.

3.   His Holiness the Dalai Lama and H.C. Cutler, *The Art of Happiness: A handbook for living*, Hodder: Sydney, 2005, p. 77.

4.   N. Burrell, C. Hill, and M. Allen, 'A Meta-Analysis of Demand/Withdraw Communication in Marriage', *All Academic, Inc*, 2008. <http://citation.allacademic.com//meta/p_mla_apa_research_citation/2/5/8/1/5/pages258159/p258159-19.php> (10 August 2013).

5.   K. Neff, *Self-Compassion: The proven power of being kind to yourself*, Harper Collins, New York, 2011, pp. 6–8.

6.   S. Salzberg, *Lovingkindness: The revolutionary art of happiness*, Shambala: Boston, 1995, pp. 111.

Chapter 3—Mindfulness of our thinking

1.   B. Khoury, T. Lecomte, G. Fortin, M. Masse, P. Therien, V. Bouchard, M. Chapleau, K. Paquin, and S. Hofman, 'Mindfulness-based therapy: A comprehensive meta-analysis', *Clinical Pyschology Review*, 2013, vol. 33, pp. 763–71.

2.   N.I. Eisenberger, M.D. Lieberman, and K.D. Williams, 'Does rejection hurt? An fMRI study of social exclusion', *Science*, 2003, vol. 302, pp. 290–2.

3.   F.D. Fincham, 'Attributions in close relationships: From Balkanization to integration', in G.J.O. Fletcher and M.S. Clark (eds), *Blackwell Handbook of Social Psychology: Interpersonal processes*, Malden, MA: Blackwell, 2001, pp. 3–31.

4.   Z. Pearce and W. Halford, 'Do attributions mediate the association between attachment and negative couple communication?', *Personal Relationships*, 2008, vol. 15, pp. 155–70.

5. J.M., Gottman, *Why Marriages Succeed or Fail*, Simon & Schuster: New York, 1994, p. 29.

6. K.A. McGonagle, R.C. Kessler and E.A. Schilling, 'The frequency and determinants of marital disagreements in a community sample', *Journal of Social and Personal Relationships*, 1992, vol. 9, pp. 507–24.

7. R.S. Miller, *Intimate Relationships* (6th edn), McGraw-Hill: New York, 2009, p. 22.

8. C.R. Agnew, P.A.M. Van Lange, C.E. Rusbult and C.A. Langston, 'Cognitive interdependence: Commitment and the mental representation of close relationships', *Journal of Personality and Social Psychology*, 2004, vol. 74, pp. 939–54.

9. M. Ritter, 'Essence of Valentine's Day, love, still a psychological puzzle', *Associated Press*, 1985. <www.apnewsarchive.com/1985/ Essence-of-Valentine-s-Day-Love-Still-A-Psychological-Puzzle/id-ec8bc242be-28d31896a4213601d326f5> (10 August 2013).

Chapter 5—Anger

1. E.A. Impett, S.L. Gable and L.A. Peplau, 'Giving up and giving in: The costs and benefits of daily sacrifice in intimate relationships', *Journal of Personality and Social Psychology*, 2005, vol. 89, pp. 327–44.

2. Thich Nhat Hanh, *Anger: Buddhist wisdom for cooling the flames*, Rider: London, 2001, pp. 23–4, 56–60.

3. A. Solzhenitsyn, *The Gulag Archipelago: 1918–1956: An Experiment in Literary Investigation*, vol. II, Harper & Row: New York, 1975, pp. 615–17.

4. J.M. Lohr, B.O. Olatunji, R.F. Baumeister and B.J. Bushman, 'The psychology of anger venting and empirically supported alternatives that do not harm', *Scientific Review of Mental Health Practice*, 2007, vol. 5, pp. 53–64.

5. J. Gottman, *Why Marriages Succeed or Fail*, Simon & Schuster: New York, 1994, p. 58.

6. J. Kornfield, *The Wise Heart: A guide to the universal teachings of Buddhist Psychology*, Bantam Books: New York, 2008, pp. 102–6.

Chapter 6—Housework

1. D.G. Myers, *Social Psychology* (9th edn), McGraw Hill: New York, 2008, pp. 62–3, 67.

2. J. Coleman, *The Lazy Husband: How to get men to do more parenting and housework*, St Martin's Press: New York, 2005, pp. 1–71.

3. S. Maushart, *Wifework: What marriage really means for women*, Text Publishing: Melbourne, 2001, pp. 237, 87.

4. T. Jones, 'Wifework set to enter feminist lexicon', *Australian Broadcasting Corporation: Lateline*, 2001 <www.abc.net.au/lateline/stories/s289890.htm> (10 August 2013).

Chapter 7—Communication

1. Marshall B. Rosenberg, <www.youtube.com/watch?v=XBGlF7-MPFI> (10 August 2013), (talk, San Francisco, April 2000).

Chapter 8—Reducing stress and anxiety

1. G. Claxton, *The Heart of Buddhism: Practical wisdom for an agitated world*, Crucible: Cornwall, 1990, pp. 38, 39, 121.

Chapter 9—Who is our partner?

1. G. Claxton, *The Heart of Buddhism: Practical wisdom for an agitated world*, Crucible: Cornwall, 1990, p. 71.

2. S.D. Kilpatrick, V.L. Bissonnette and C.E. Rusbult, 'Empathic accuracy and accommodative behaviour among newly married couples', *Personal Relationships*, 2002, vol. 9, pp. 369–93.

3. G. Kramer, *Insight Dialogue: The interpersonal path to freedom*, Shambhala: Boston, 2007, p. 40. More information about Insight Dialogue practice, retreats, and online resources can be found at the website, <www.metta.org>.

4. 'Husband's willingness to be influenced by wife, share power are key predictors of newlywed happiness, stability', *UW Today*, 1998 <www.washington.edu/news/1998/02/20/husbands-willingness-to-be-influenced-by-wife-share-power-are-key-predictors-of-newlywed-happiness-stability-uw-study-shows/> (10 August 2013).

5. J. Kornfield, *The Wise Heart: A guide to the universal teachings of Buddhist psychology*, Bantam Books: New York, 2008, pp. 12–13.

6. S. Maushart, *Wifework: What marriage really means for women*, Text Publishing: Melbourne, 2001, p. 209.

Chapter 10—Sex

1. B. Arndt, *The Sex Diaries: Why women go off sex and other bedroom battles*, Melbourne University Press: Melbourne, 2009, pp. 6–7, 35.

2. M. Weiner Davis, *The Sex-starved Marriage: Boosting your marriage libido*, Simon & Schuster: London, 2003, pp. 8, 36, 53.

3. R. Basson, S. Leiblum, L. Brotto, L. Derogatis, J. Fourcroy, et al., 'Definitions of women's sexual dysfunction reconsidered: Advocating expansion and revision', *Journal of Psychosomatic Obstetrics & Gynaecology*, 2003, vol. 24, no. 4, pp. 221–9.
4. S. Maushart, *Wifework: What marriage really means for women*, Text Publishing: Melbourne, 2001, pp. 231–2.
5. D. Schnarch, *Passionate Marriage: Keeping love and intimacy alive in committed relationships*, W. W. Norton & Company: New York, 2009, pp. 78–9.

Chapter 11—Infidelity

1. M.A. Tafoya and B.H. Spitzberg, 'The dark side of infidelity: Its nature, prevalence, and communicative functions', in B.H. Spitzberg and W.R. Cupach (eds), *The Dark Side of Interpersonal Communication* (2nd edn), Mahwah, NJ: Lawrence Erlbaum Associates, 2007, pp. 201–42.
2. R. Sachs, *The Passionate Buddha: Wisdom on intimacy and enduring love*, Inner Traditions: Rochester, VT, 2002, pp. 191–3.
3. J. Kabat-Zinn, *Wherever You Go, There You Are: Mindfulness meditation in everyday life*, Hyperion: New York, 1995.
4. J. Kornfield, *The Wise Heart: A guide to the universal teachings of Buddhist psychology*, Bantam Books: New York, 2008, p. 193.

Chapter 12—Tolerance of difficult behaviour

1. J. Fitness, 'Emotion and communication in families', in A. Vangelisti (ed.), *Handbook of Family Communication*, Lawrence Erlbaum Associates: Mahwah, NJ, 2004, p. 483.
2. C.E. Rusbult, J. Verette, G.A. Whitney, L.F. Slovik and I. Lipkus, 'Accommodation processes in close relationships: Theory and preliminary empirical evidence', *Journal of Personality and Social Psychology*, 1991, vol. 60, pp. 53–78.
3. D.R. Peterson, 'Conflict', in H.H. Kelley, E. Berscheid, A. Christenen et al. (eds), *Close Relationships*, Percheron Press: Clinton Corners, NY, 2002, p. 382.
4. L. Doyle, *The Surrendered Wife: A practical guide to finding intimacy, passion, and peace with a man*, Fireside: New York, 2001, pp. 18–19.

Chapter 13—Forgiveness and understanding

1. M. Weiner Davis, *The Sex-starved Marriage: Boosting your marriage libido*, Simon & Schuster: London, 2003, p. 53.
2. S. Salzberg, *Lovingkindness: The revolutionary art of happiness*, Shambala: Boston, 1995, p. 93.

3. Integrated Behavioral Couples Therapy: Review of Jacobson and Christenson's model of Couples Therapy, *PsychPage*, 2013, <www.psychpage.com/family/library/ibct.html> (11 March 2013).

Chapter 14—Turning things around

1. J.M. Gottman and R.W. Levenson, 'Marital processes predictive of later dissolution: Behaviour, physiology, and health', *Journal of Personality and Social Psychology*, 1992, vol. 63, pp. 221–33.
2. S.L. Gable, H.T. Reis and G. Downey, 'He said, she said: A quasi-signal detection analysis of daily interactions between close relationship partners', *Psychological Science*, 2003, vol. 14, pp. 100–5.
3. R. Hanson and R. Mendius, *Buddha's Brain: The practical neuroscience of happiness, love and wisdom*, New Harbinger Publications, Inc.: Oakland, CA, 2009, pp. 68–76.
4. E.F. Loftus, and D.M. Bernstein, 'Rich false memories: The royal road to success', in A.F. Healy (ed.), *Experimental cognitive psychology and its applications*, Washington, DC: American Psychological Association, 2005, p. 81.
5. D. Holmberg and J.G. Holmes, 'Reconstruction of relationship memories: A mental models approach', in N. Schwarz and S. Sudman (eds), *Autobiographical Memory and the Validity of Retrospective Reports*, New York: Springer-Velag, 1994, p. 82.
6. ABC Television, *Making Couples Happy*, Sydney, 2013.

Chapter 15—Being authentic and present with our partner

1. K. Armstrong, 'Kristin Armstrong on Marriage', *Glamour Weddings*, 2006. <www.glamour.com/weddings/2006/07/kristin-armstrong?currentPage=2> (10 August 2013).
2. L. and C. Bloom, *101 Things I Wish I Knew When I Got Married: Simple lessons to make love last*, New World Library: Novato, CA, 2004, pp. 87–9.

Chapter 16—Cultivating love

1. J. Kornfield, *The Art of Forgiveness, Lovingkindness and Peace*, Bantam: New York, 2002, p. 73.
2. S. Dowrick, *The Almost-Perfect Marriage: One-minute relationship skills*, Allen & Unwin: Sydney, 2007, pp. 26, 138.
3. Thich Nhat Hanh, *Teachings on Love*, Parallax Press: Berkeley, CA, 1998, p. 117.

4. F. Strack, L. Martin and S. Stepper, 'Inhibiting and facilitating conditions of the human smile: A nonobtrusive test of the facial feedback hypothesis', *Journal of Personality and Social Psychology,* 1988, vol. 54, pp. 768–77.

5. P.R. Amato, A. Booth, D.R. Johnson and S.J. Rogers, *Alone Together: How marriage in America is changing*, Cambridge, MA: Harvard University Press, 2007, p. 186.

index